Attracting
Purple Martins

Attracting Purple Martins

By J. L. Wade

*New advice from the man who made
the purple martin a household word —
the results of 20 years of attracting and
caring for "America's most wanted bird."*

The Nature Society
1987

Copyright 1987, by J. L. Wade

Published by
The Nature Society
Purple Martin Junction
Griggsville, Illinois 62340

Color plate, opposite page:
"Purple Martin," Plate 1 of
collector series by Richard Sloan
Copyright 1968 by J. L. Wade.

Library of Congress Cataloging-in-Publication Data:

Wade, J. L., 1913-
    Attracting Purple Martins

    1. Purple martin. 2. Birds, Protection of.
3. Birds, Attracting of.   I. Title
QL696.P247W33 1987   639.9'78813   86-28554

ISBN 0-9616774-0-6

Printed in The United States of America
First printing 1987
Second printing 1988
Third printing 1990
Fourth printing 1991
Fifth printing 1994
Sixth printing 2002

Dedication

This book is gratefully dedicated to the hundreds of purple martin enthusiasts who are mentioned by name in its pages...and to the other thousands who are not.

Contents

Contents

Section A: THE GRIGGSVILLE STORY

Includes the first four chapters dealing with history of the project, and issues closely associated with it, including the mosquito question.

Describes how the Griggsville interest originated; development of modern housing; early successes.

Tells how the bird was promoted and Griggsville became active on both commercial and non-commercial fronts.

Recounts in detail one of the more interesting episodes in the early promotion of the bird.

Recaps this issue and surveys the best supporting evidence for the martin as a mosquito-eater.

Section B: THE PURPLE MARTIN STORY

Includes a seven-chapter natural history of the species, the most detailed discussion yet published of all aspects of its life cycle.

Describes the physical attributes of this species, and a variety of other biological information.

Introduction

Now, in 1986, well over 20 years after the martins began coming to the houses of Griggsville and I began writing my first book, seems a good time to pause and reflect on what the past two decades have accomplished.

My first book, "What You Should Know About the Purple Martin," was started during the era of "Silent Spring," when Rachel Carson's famous 1963 book on the dangers of chemicals in the environment started a whole nation talking. In my original foreword, I wondered whether there is some mechanism built into humans that causes them to pause after a great technological leap forward and let their physical evolution catch up with their brainstorms. This was definitely a time of changing perspective, when humans were beginning to look — or try to look — at the whole picture that they had created with the chemical revolution.

This was a fertile time for the people of Griggsville, because the nation listened to the purple martin story, and acted. Martin houses began to go up as never before, and a great many people found themselves drawn into an interest that extended far beyond martins to all the wild birds of the continent.

That initial excitement lasted only a few years, but the public's interest has never returned to its previous low level. While these mosquito-eating swallows no longer have the novelty value many writers gave them in the '60s, they are much better known today, and enthusiasts are legion. Martins have taken their place among regular subjects of nature writers in the media.

On a broader level, concern about pollution has spread into every part of our society, and is so pervasive it would be difficult to measure in this one brief foreword. Environmental issues range from mild concerns to intense and often angry controversies. While many injustices and economic mistakes have been made in the name of conservation, I believe the balance of this concern has been for the better. There is no doubt some of our industrial activities if allowed to go unregulated would ruin our environment, and without a healthy environment, we have no future.

In 1966, many persons asked why a whole book devoted to purple martins. The answer was simple. Public interest existed, and prior to that book no single volume drew together all information needed to satisfy that curiosity.

Prior to that first book, martins had not really been ignored in ornithological writings. In fact, many of history's finest had contributed greatly to our knowledge. But natural history is a science with few static truths. Every species has unanswered questions, and the seemingly minor observation of any observer can cast a new light on what had been considered a valid conclusion by scientists.

During the past 20 years we have worked with tens of thousands of those individual observers — the purple martin landlords of North America — and helped them share experiences. Our original book was a blend of ornithological references and backyard observations, and this one is, too.

We aren't the only ones who benefit from the observations of these backyard observers. For 20 years we have published a newspaper loaded with their letters, and many researchers read it as avidly as anyone else, looking for valuable pieces of information.

During the past two decades, scientists have expanded the study of the martins, and there is now a larger body of writings on specific questions than we can even suggest here. Even so, some questions remain as much puzzles as ever. How many mosquitoes does a typical martin eat in a typical situation? When first scouts leave a house for a week or so, where do they go? Why will martins take eggshells or grit from a feeder, but not survival food when cold weather eliminates their normal food supply? And so on.

This book won't answer all existing questions about martins, but we're sure of one thing: You will find here the best information available on attracting these birds — and the best information on why you will be glad you did.

Section A

The Griggsville Story

Chapter 1

How It All Began

The story of Griggsville and the purple martin started with a Jaycee project in 1962. In the following years it involved — in Griggsville alone — Boy Scouts, school classes, community park board, Western Illinois Fair board, businessmen, farmers, orchardists and municipal officials — and finally a variety of public officials, conservationists and civic volunteers throughout eastern North America.

During the past two decades, hundreds of organizations and thousands of individuals have joined the promotion of purple martins, using materials produced in Griggsville and financed with profits from martin house sales.

In 1962, the Griggsville Jaycees decided to undertake an insect-abatement program, but were hesitant to push toward more intensive use of chemical pesticides, about which there was growing confusion concerning their safety. I suggested purple martins might be the answer, because they eat nothing but flying insects and had shown a decided inclination to live in man-made apartments right in town.

The Jaycees decided to see if they could encourage a population of birds sufficient to whip the mosquito problem. Griggsville is situated between the Illinois and Mississippi rivers, with extensive lowland sloughs just four miles away, and scores of ponds in the surrounding countryside.

My experience with martin houses convinced me that if a city-wide project were to be started and then kept in motion, something quite different from the usual martin house design would be needed. I had seen many cases in which maintenance of heavy, bulky, wooden houses had become too much work for their owners. Through neglect, such houses had fallen into disrepair and had been taken over by sparrows and starlings. The Jaycees pointed out that if they were to spearhead a program to attract birds to town, they assuredly did not want them to be more sparrows and starlings!

Furthermore, the Jaycees were few in number and busy with their personal affairs. None could spare time that would be needed to keep in proper condition the large number of houses required for such an ambitious project, if these houses were to be made of wood.

Dr. T. E. Musselman, who died in 1976 at the age of 89, was a legend in the tri-states area of Illinois, Iowa and Missouri. The advice which led to the original Trio-Musselman martin house, and his 40 years of pioneering bluebird work, were just two chapters in a lifetime of work for wildlife.

Twenty-eight houses were erected on Griggsville's Quincy Street in 1963 and within a few years had made it one of the best-known main streets in America. After 23 years, the houses are still there, still hosting purple martins.

We consulted experts, including Dr. T. E. Musselman, a well known naturalist of nearby Quincy. What was needed, Dr. Musselman said, was a martin house that would attract martins, discourage sparrows and starlings, could be easily raised and lowered vertically, would require practically no upkeep and, finally, offer living conditions conducive to the health and welfare of newly hatched martins.

From these suggestions, our company's design engineers fashioned a prototype of a 12-compartment, two-story aluminum house. It incorporated features to meet the requirements outlined by Dr. Musselman plus other innovations that occurred as development proceeded.

Dr. Musselman was so pleased with the functional design of the new unit he asked that the martin house carry his name. The Trio-Musselman martin house, which was to help revolutionize the wild bird world, was born.

At that point, neither the purple martin nor the new house about which Dr. Musselman, the Jaycees, and I were so enthusiastic had proved itself in Griggsville.

Nature House furnished the Jaycees with 28 of the new houses at nominal cost, and chapter members installed these on telescoping steel posts previously erected at 100-ft. intervals along the city's main thoroughfare, Quincy Street. At the same time, the Jaycees began a campaign urging other citizens to install houses. The deluxe accommodations were ready and waiting when the martins arrived in the spring of 1963.

Results were noticeable that first season, and were beyond expectations in several ways. Remarkably, house occupancy was approximately 80 percent — 22 of the 28 houses attracted martins — and the Quincy Street colony began to flourish instantly. (Several owners of older wooden houses complained their martins had deserted them to take up residence in the new apartments!) Word that there was ample housing in Griggsville evidently spread among the martins in the area, because the city attracted many more martins than had ever been noticed here before.

When the martins arrived, effect on mosquito and other insect populations was immediately apparent. Townspeople, once again able to enjoy their lawns and gardens without annoyance from flying pests, were lavish in their praise for the martins.

When the martins left for the south that autumn, the Jaycees made the rounds, cleaning out old nests and closing the houses for the winter. They discovered some sparrow nests in the new houses, but not one starling had attempted to build a nest in any of them. In 23 years, we have never found a starling nest in any of the regular houses either uptown or at Purple Martin Junction, although starlings did nest a few years ago in a very large (and somewhat darker) experimental compartment in a house at the Junction.

During various inspection tours by the Jaycees during the nesting season, they noted no fatalities among young martins in any of the aluminum houses. These facts were clear proof that the design and material concepts of the house were sound.

With success of the insect abatement program recognized by the Griggsville citizenry, the Jaycees expanded their project in the spring of 1964. Additional houses were installed at other locations.

Among these were a dozen installed at the beginning of June on the grounds of the Western Illinois Fair, an annual week-long event held in Griggsville since 1887. It was the fair that provided the martins' first big test and the first striking proof of their effectiveness in controlling insects in a concentrated area.

Insects had been a headache for fair manager J. R. Skinner. For 17 years Skinner had used chemical insecticides on the grounds in an effort to alleviate the problem of the flies, gnats and mosquitoes that "bugged" fair patrons, stockmen and concessionaires.

"Every year we tried the latest thing in insecticides, pesticides, sprays," he said. "We ruined food by spraying. Horsemen complained their animals became sick grazing in fields that had been sprayed. And the best result we got with insect sprays was a four-day kill — provided we were lucky and it didn't rain.

"But when we started getting martins," he continued, "we quit having flies and mosquitoes. It came time to do our annual spraying before the fair, and we didn't have to do any. The martins were at work all over the grounds."

But the real test came after the fair. Columnist Clarissa Start told it best in an article that appeared in the Feb. 20, 1965 St. Louis Post-Dispatch. An excerpt from that feature, which helped bring the Griggsville story to prominence, relates:

"Ordinarily, when the tents come down the flies and mosquitoes really take over, and people complain that they cannot go to the park in comfort. The fair committee had ordered $600 worth of pesticides. Something happened to the shipment; it was sidetracked at another town and didn't arrive. But the martins did arrive, not only the Griggsville resident martins, but hundreds of others.

"'One day I looked out the window and the place was loaded with martins', said Skinner. 'They were on top of the grandstand, they were lined up along the wires. They were perched on an antenna as if it were a launching pad. It was unbelievable. They must have sent out the call to martins for miles around.'

"The result was the flies and mosquitoes were cleaned out. When the chemical firm's troubleshooter arrived to explain the delay in shipment, the fair committee said they were sorry but they wouldn't need the sprays.

"'We told him if he could find a fly or mosquito on the premises we'd order 10 times as much spray,' said Skinner. 'He couldn't. He was very nice about it and took the order back. I still say if I hadn't seen it with my own eyes, I wouldn't have believed it.'"

Until 1964, the Griggsville experiment was relatively unknown outside the community's immediate area. That changed rapidly in 1964 and 1965.

A cartoon extolling the virtues of the purple martin appeared on the front page of the April 17, 1964 Chicago Tribune. Richard Curry, president of the Jaycees, wrote a letter to the Tribune describing the success of the Griggsville project. Publication of his letter drew regional attention to "The Purple Martin Capital of the World." The Jaycees were deluged with letters from people throughout the midwest, encouraging them in their project and wanting more information about it.

Early in 1965, Clarissa Start's article appeared, and since then many newspapers, magazines and electronic news services have reported extensively on the Griggsville story. Millions of words have appeared in all parts of the U.S. and Canada (and overseas, too), and have made Griggsville one of the better known small towns in America.

Governor Otto Kerner declared an official "Purple Martin Time in Illinois" in 1965.

Effects of the project on Griggsville would fill a book. More and more houses were put up, and Nature House was soon mass producing them in addition to its regular lines of television antennas and lawn and garden products. In 1965, Griggsville erected a 40-ft., 504-compartment martin tower in the center of the city as a focal point for visitor interest. The media quickly dubbed it "the Empire State Building of the bird world."

In a Chicago Motor Club booklet that year, Griggsville was one of 87 points of interest in Illinois. That booklet, first of many recognitions by travel organizations, said:

"GRIGGSVILLE (pop. 1,240, alt. 674 ft.) A serious mosquito problem and the town's location along the Brazil-Illinois migration route of the purple martin led Griggsville to put the two together in an unusual program of natural insect control. About 120 martin houses are occupied from the birds' arrival in March until their departure in the autumn. Since each martin devours approximately 2,000 flying insects daily, the mosquitoes have been almost eliminated."

Since the Griggsville example, many other communities have tried it. In addition, many communities and mosquito control districts became more conscious of nature in general and the many other life forms that work to control mosquitoes. I believe we have caused many authorities to realize that nature must still do the lion's share of keeping each species in check and that any chemical insecticide must always be a supplementary and carefully used control factor.

Chapter 2

It's Purple Martin Time!

Once the citizens of Griggsville had proved to themselves the effectiveness of the purple martin in natural insect control, they set out to promote the bird throughout the nation. Some of our methods were as orthodox as writing letters to newspaper editors. Others were as unorthodox as the classified ad placed by the Jaycees in the New Orleans Times-Picayune of March 8, 1964. The ad, which surprisingly did get several responses, but none from persons who could deliver by the specified date, said:

"Mosquitoes Urgently Needed. Jaycees of Griggsville, Illinois, need 500,000 live mosquitoes delivered healthy and active by March 26. Must be in flying condition. Highest prices paid. Inquire promptly to Jaycees, Griggsville, Illinois. Phone 164."

Maud O'Bryan, the paper's want ad reporter, remarked in her column of that date, "Are mosquitoes livestock? They are to the Jaycees of Griggsville, Illinois, who sent an ad wanting 500,000 live mosquitoes — and ordered it to run under 'Wanted to Buy — Livestock.'

"A half-million mosquitoes must be delivered healthy and active and in perfect flying condition by March 26. What for? Your guess is as good as ours. The price per mosquito? Ditto....If you find out what they are going to do with a half-million flying mosquitoes, let us know..."

The columnist got her answer from George Mobus, who had placed the ad for the Jaycees. He explained the town had put up 28 houses for purple martins the year before and had become known as the "purple martin town."

"One purple martin will eat 2,000 mosquitoes in a day," he said. "Griggsville was mosquito-less last summer. It was able to give a street dance in August till midnight — and the purple martins stayed up to watch the people dance.

"This spring," Mobus continued, "purple martins are sending scouts to find where the eating is good. Several martins have arrived in Griggsville, but there are no mosquitoes this early in the season. Jaycees want to roll out the red carpet for the scouts with some choice, juicy Louisiana mosquitoes, but so far the ad has not produced that half-million required to feed 250 martins for one day."

In just three years, that figure of 2,000 mosquitoes per day became established in purple martin literature and was automatically quoted whenever the bird's name was mentioned anywhere in the country. There is some irony in the figure as I will explain a bit later, but first let me explain how it came to be a part of modern martin literature.

I originated the figure after extensive study of the martin's feeding habits, and when I settled on it I felt it was very conservative. My studies had shown that a martin must as an average consume its own body weight in insects each day. That average weight is two ounces, and this equals around 7,000 mosquitoes.

Many common bird species must individually consume several thousands of a particular insect daily in order to survive. In her book, "Gardening Without Poisons," Beatrice Trum Hunter had written, "A house wren feeds 500 spiders and caterpillars to its young during one summer afternoon. A swallow devours 1,000 leafhoppers in 12 hours. A pair of flickers consider 5,000 ants a mere snack. A Baltimore oriole consumes 17 hairy caterpillars a minute. A brown thrasher can eat over 6,000 insects a day."

I had little doubt a purple martin could consume its weight in mosquitoes each day, but martins are not extremely selective eaters, and will eat whatever is available, including flies, dragonflies, beetles, moths, locusts, weevils and miscellaneous other airborne bits of life. A martin's diet is seldom confined for very long to any one insect species and works to eliminate from its immediate area a large percentage of almost all types of flying insects.

The martin's short, triangular beak opens into a relatively large cavity which the bird uses as a "scoop" as it darts through the air, snatching large insects or gathering in large numbers of small ones much as a whale's cavernous mouth scoops up enormous numbers of tiny sea creatures. A sticky substance coats the inside of the martin's mouth, and tiny insects are irretrievably trapped therein. A martin may then swallow them or compress them into a pellet which it carries to its young in the nest.

Although I felt the estimate of 2,000 mosquitoes per day was conservative, it came as a startling claim to millions of persons who were not used to thinking in terms of the thousands of insects which individuals of many species eat in a single day. Citizens still were not fully aware of the gigantic job of insect control performed by all of our wild bird species nor of the speed with which the earth would be lost to insect hordes if birds were absent from our environment. "Two thousand mosquitoes per day" thus became the keynote phrase of a rapidly mushrooming campaign to focus attention on the martin.

In the following years, controversy developed over that figure, partly

In 1965 I picked up the title of "purple martin king" after this presentation at the annual meeting in Indianapolis of the National Association for the Protection and Propagation of Purple Martins and Bluebirds of America (NAPPPMBA). A plaque, presented by T. E. Musselman (left), was given honoring our promotional efforts of the early '60s in bringing the martin favorable public attention.

because some persons were reluctant to believe martins do eat mosquitoes, and partly, I believe, because some chemical-oriented mosquito control officials felt threatened. Critics pointed to a pair of stomach analysis studies that showed few mosquitoes in the stomachs of those sample birds, but the background data on these studies were so slight they were virtually meaningless to this particular question.

These same critics too easily dismissed the case of a single martin killed in early morning hours that had already consumed 300 mosquitoes. But more about this issue later.

For the moment, suffice it to point out that this phrase became very widely discussed and contributed enormously to the current interest in martins. Consequently, it came as a note of irony and startling coincidence when, in 1983, nearly 20 years after we first used it, we learned another purple martin promoter, Joseph Dodson of Kankakee, Illinois had used the same phrase. He had originated it in his literature in the 1920s, and claimed to have based it on the analysis of an actual stomach. I'll discuss the Dodson case in detail in Chapter 4.

By the spring of 1966, the Griggsville Wild Bird Society was on the scene. This organization, that later was to become the Nature Society, was sponsored by Trio Manufacturing Company (that later was to become Nature House, Inc.). Led by Chairman A. E. Vail, the Society promoted all birds, but its original members joined because of their interest in martins. The Society immediately began collecting and distributing information about birds.

Although active in 1965, their presence on the continental scene was not felt until 1966. Before that spring and summer were past, the Society had made a unique mark on the midwest and south and its influence was beginning to be felt far and wide.

In 1965, the Society prepared material for a 13-1/2 minute movie. "The Purple Martin Story," which was released early in 1966, has been shown to television, school and civic club audiences in thousands of locations and is still in circulation. The movie was produced entirely by Griggsville citizens. George Mobus wrote the script, Wayne Bradshaw shot more than 5,000 feet of film to collect the 400 feet which eventually were used, and "Red" Stead of Stead Sound Service recorded the sound.

Rex Davis, a martin enthusiast and one of the most popular radio personalities in St. Louis, narrated the film.

Early in 1966, the Purple Martin Capital News began publication as the link between the Griggsville Wild Bird Society and its members. It eventually became the Nature Society News, but not until 1979, three years after the organization itself had changed its name to the Nature Society. The name of the purple martin may have finally dropped out of its flag, but to its staff and readers it is still "the purple martin paper."

As interest in martins grew, stores joined in the excitement. This display was in a Smith and Welton department store window in Norfolk, Virginia, in the early '70s. For the first time ever, a birdhouse had become an important commercial product.

The News was originated to solve a problem. Griggsville was deluged with more letters than could be personally answered during those early years and we finally conceived the News as a way of distributing information to lots of people in a hurry. Many people who wrote to Griggsville in the mid-60s found themselves receiving a newspaper every month, with our hope the answer to their question was somewhere in it.

We loaded the News with letters and established a uniqueness which prevails today. During a typical 12 months the News publishes approximately 500 letters, several hundred migration reports, and miscellaneous other material from members. This policy has made it a forum for the Society, and drawn backyard bird enthusiasts everywhere together into a community of interest.

From the beginning the News has reflected an interest broader than martins, but that was intensified in January, 1986, when the paper expanded its primary coverage to include all native songbirds. Without sacrificing any of our martin interest, we set out to do as much for other popular birds as we have done for martins, and the reception among readers has been exciting.

My first book, "What You Should Know About the Purple Martin," was also published in 1966.

But the most striking activities of the Society that year were the promotions held in Houston, St. Louis and Chicago. In all these cities, Purple Martin Time met enthusiastic acceptance by city administrations, civic groups, business people and media. They pushed interest in wild birds to its highest level in years.

Although the eventual reaction of virtually everyone was wholehearted approval, initial reactions of some people, especially media representatives, were curiosity, skepticism, hilarity, or all of these, depending on the situation. Chicago, the largest inland population center in the nation, is alleged to be a mecca for con artists, and brand new ideas are often met with raised eyebrows. The Chicago Sun-Times raised its eyebrow on page 3 with the headline, "Cackle Goes Up For Purple Martins," and kicked off the story with, "Monday morning was the first full day of spring and the sounds of public relations men could be heard in the land."

The Chicago Tribune printed several stories on the opening of Purple Martin Time, with leads like that on a story by Edward Schreiber which read, "J. L. Wade came by the way from Griggsville, Pike County, to Mayor Daley's office yesterday to sing the praises of purple martins — and the purple martini."

The Sun-Times editorialized — giving the promotion the benefit of the doubt but apparently still not too certain that it was on the level: "If Purple Martin Time is inspired by promotion, then it's a harmless enough sales pitch, perhaps, and may even have its nonprofit benefits. Somebody's got to provide a home for the birds."

Other Chicago newspapers and radio and television stations soon joined the celebration. Martin Wyant wrote in the Tribune, "Move over, Rover! A bird is bucking for status as man's best friend.

"'It's Purple Martin Time,' the Griggsville Wild Bird Society is proclaiming in Chicago today thru next Saturday.

"The spring festival for 'man's best summer friend' is the third sponsored by the society this year. The first two festivals, in Houston and St. Louis, have already been successful, as the martins touched down in these cities right on schedule in their annual springtime flight from the Amazon valley of Brazil."

It had all started in Houston, where the Gulf Coast Horticultural Society sponsored the event, and in Texarkana, Texas where the Camellia Garden Club whipped up enthusiasm for the birds.

In Houston, Mayor Louie Welch issued a proclamation designating February 6-12 as Purple Martin Time, and in Texarkana, Mayor Neal Courtney proclaimed Purple Martin Time to begin March 1.

Houston, the nation's sixth largest city then (it's now fourth) and a world aerospace center, became preoccupied for a week, not with big metal birds but with small feathered ones.

The Gulf Coast Horticultural Society passed out Purple Martin Time buttons, presented a new martin Castle to the city, distributed literature to the news media, and took advantage of every opportunity to tell the birds' story.

The Griggsville organization distributed place mats and cocktail napkins depicting the martin's virtues. Purple martinis appeared in a number of Houston lounges. Banners proclaiming Purple Martin Time appeared in store windows, and motel and theater marquees followed suit.

Purple martin houses began to go up in the Houston area in unprecedented numbers.

Houston's enthusiasm was duplicated in St. Louis. The ball was carried by the East Central District of Federated Garden Clubs, which presented Castles to the City of St. Louis and Forest Park Zoo. The zoo Castle, accepted by Marlin Perkins, director and narrator of the syndicated television feature, "Wild Kingdom," was to figure more than once in the news.

On April 19 it was stolen. The Castle, valued at $75 (remember, this was 1966) was taken — pole, concrete mounting block and all — long with a terrace light valued at $200, from its location near the Jewel Box in Forest Park.

The stolen Castle was replaced by the Wild Bird Society and soon was back in the news. Several martin families moved in and provided, according to the St. Louis Globe-Democrat, "the zoo's first volunteer exhibit."

In Chicago, the Garden Club of Illinois did a masterful job in behalf of the birds. Members distributed lapel pins and literature throughout the city and at their World Flower Show exhibit at McCormick Place, where it was exposed to approximately 370,000 visitors.

Purple Martin Time in Chicago was March 20-27, which occurred during the city's most eventful period of 1966. The little purple martin battled for the spotlight with such formidable competitors as Prince Phillip, Vice President Humphrey, Martin Luther King and St. Patrick. When it was over, the martin had shoved its broad little shoulders into the number one spot. For weeks afterward, it was a favorite conversation item among disc jockeys of the city.

An unusual aspect of the three major promotions is that, in each locality, the first martin scouts verified their reputations for punctuality by arriving very close to opening day. The cliff swallow is noted for amazing predictability, having gained fame for its return to San Juan Capistrano on pretty much the same date each year, but the martin has not been noted for the same regularity.

When the Society asked me for the most favorable dates on which to schedule the promotions in these cities, we consulted arrival records for

The "Sixties surge" of purple martin interest reached as far as New Brunswick in the extreme northeast where this group met in 1968 to form the New Brunswick Purple Martin and Bird Society. Today, they're still going strong, with a membership in the hundreds and interests that range over the whole world of birds. Many other local clubs have been inspired by the purple martin interest during the past two decades.

these areas and discovered that arrival dates of first scouts from year to year appeared to be more consistent than arrivals of the main flocks. We have since come to believe the reverse may be true, but at the time we went ahead with a great deal of confidence and selected dates we felt would be very close to actual dates first scouts would be sighted. The dates turned out to be remarkably accurate.

Houston observed Purple Martin Time during the week of Feb. 6-12, and the first scouts appeared there Feb. 7. St. Louis held the event March 13-20 and the first sighting was March 13. Chicago celebrated March 20-27, and the first scout was reported three days prior to the opening, on March 17.

Many other successful promotions were held in the '60s. One of them — in Cleveland in 1968 — was featured by the prestigious Housewares Review magazine, which singled out the promotion as one of the "all-time market makers" and cited the unusual public benefits tied to the promotion. All of the sponsors — City of Cleveland, Garden Clubs of Ohio, Halle Brothers Department Stores and Griggsville Wild Bird Society — were cited for their parts in creating an especially unusual and worthwhile event.

The commercial promotion of the martin house also benefited from the work of some of the nation's leading industrial and retail organizations.

The Cotter Company, a Chicago-based organization that then served more than 3,000 home-owned True Value hardware stores (and now serves more than twice that number), was the first to take advantage of the martin's rising status as a true sign of spring. Cotter keyed its entire two-page 1966 spring promotion in Look magazine to the purple martin, printing the background in shades of purple, carrying the martin house as a lead item, and headlining the ad, "EARLY BIRD SPECIALS! Get set for Spring — and the Purple Martins, too!"

In February, 1966, the Moorman Manufacturing Company, one of the nation's largest makers of livestock feed concentrates, offered Trio martin houses as a premium item to its customers. When it was over, 9,500 martin houses had been sold in a single month!

Paul Cory, then vice president of marketing for Moorman's, attributed acceptance among farmers to the fact that, "It reminds them that their fathers and grandfathers all had martins around their homes, not only to provide entertainment, but to chase hawks away from their chickens, crows away from their crops, and free their livestock from being bothered by insects."

Farmers were naturally quickest to understand that a particular type of birdhouse could aid survival of young birds, too. That seemed obvious to us, but turned out to be widely regarded as unique. Apparently, it had not occurred to most people that fundamentals known to American livestock people for decades could be applied to wildlife as well.

The late Charles Butler of Arkansas City, Kansas, then vice president of the National Association for the Protection and Propagation of Purple Martins and Bluebirds of America, Inc. (NAPPPMBA) had had a large colony for many years. In 1965, he replaced his large windmill-style house with aluminum houses.

"At first I thought it was a big mistake," he said. "When my birds began to arrive, they took a look around for the windmill and then flew right on by. But they came back eventually, and now there are only two empty compartments among the 60."

Butler said he believed the Trio aluminum houses were the greatest thing that had happened to the purple martin. The greatest advantage for the birds was that modern houses kept a greater number of his young alive. In the summer of 1966, Butler said, ". . .it has produced the most birds I have ever had, I believe, per nesting unit. . .I believe I can truthfully say I have at least 250 birds, making an increase of two young to each nesting place."

Since then we have heard that sentiment echoed over and over.

The ultimate and most vital benefit, however, is that which is accruing to **all** birds as a result of the growing awareness of all of nature's creatures. The case is summed up in this excerpt from a Decatur, Illinois, Herald article ("Martins Have Efficient Allies") which is as fitting today as it was in 1965:

"Behind the enthusiasm for housing purple martins and an effort in the General Assembly to make the martin the official state bird. . .is one valid concern. The martin is an avid mosquito-eater.

"But the energetic birds for whom their admirers erect handsome martin houses are not the only effective insect exterminators. Moreover, the natural enemies of insect pests include viruses, fungi, worms and microbes, as well as other insects. Our small neighbors live — and die — in a fiercely competitive world.

"In fact, if it were not for the balance of nature provided by these competitive forms of life, says E. F. Knipling, chief of the entomology division of the FDA, 'all the chemical pesticides in the world wouldn't be adequate to keep the insect world from taking over.'"

Chapter 3

The Great
State Bird Debate

The Saturday Evening Post of February 12, 1966, took a long and critical look at the condition of American state governments in 1965 in an article entitled, "Octopus in the State House." Illinois came in for a major share of criticism, most of it unfavorable. Among other things, the Post looked skeptically at the state's interest in birds. An excerpt from the article reads:

"February passed; then March and April and May. The Senate passed hundreds of 'little bills' made necessary by the lack of home rule. It decided that well diggers and tree trimmers and funeral directors had to be U.S. citizens. And it showed its concern over birds. At issue, specifically, was a bill to change the official state bird from the cardinal to the purple martin. The purple martins, it seemed, had many backers. Some Springfield bars began serving purple martinis. In the middle of the debate Chicago Sen. Anthony DeTolve — a relative by marriage of crime czar Sam (Mooney) Giancana — jumped up with an alternate suggestion. The official state bird, he cried, should be the stool pigeon."

House Bill 1058, which proposed to change the official state bird designation from the cardinal to the purple martin, was introduced by Rep. John K. Morris of Chadwick, in northern Illinois. The bill aroused no interest initially and was given an almost unanimous "do-pass" recommendation on April 14, 1965, by the Committee on Waterways, Conservation, Fish and Game. The bill had had two readings and was awaiting a final vote in the House before an appreciable segment of the state even became aware that the official status of the cardinal was in very imminent danger. A furious public debate then developed almost overnight.

Both cardinal and martin backers immediately looked toward Griggsville, both because of my previous statements concerning the purple martin and because they suspected some citizens of Griggsville of being behind the bill's introduction.

I took the floor and outlined the many benefits of the purple martin and the advantages which could accrue to the state if it were to select this bird as its symbol. I cited its voracious appetite for flying insects, its beauty and its cleanliness, its friendliness to man, the importance of the blossoming birdhouse industry to the state, and the fact that Illinois could gain a measure of uniqueness inasmuch as the martin is the official bird of no other state. Without wanting to downgrade the cardinal, I pointed out it is the symbol of seven states and, while it is beautiful and its seed-eating diet is beneficial to humans, it is of no particular importance to the state's economy. It even causes the importation of a substantial amount of sunflower seed from Kansas in the winter, I added somewhat facetiously.

Cardinal backers were indignant. They pointed out that the cardinal abides with the citizens of the state year around, while the martin leaves in the winter. They emphasized that the cardinal builds its own nest and does not depend on anyone to supply its housing, that its song is one of the most delightful of all birds, and that it is one of the most brilliantly beautiful birds in the world.

Most heated point made by the opponents, however, was that the present state bird had been selected by the school children of the state, and they felt it was not the place of the legislature to override the desires of the children.

In 1929, the Macomb branch of the National Federation of Business and Professional Women's Clubs requested that a state bird be selected and that a ballot be distributed to the school children of the state in order that they might vote. This was done.

The names of five species were printed on the ballot. A total of 128,664 votes was cast and the breakdown included:

Cardinal	39,226
Bluebird	30,306
Meadowlark	16,237
Quail	15,843
Oriole	15,449

Sixty-eight other species were written in.

As result of this school ballot, House Bill No. 5 was introduced in the 56th General Assembly by James Foster and passed on June 4, 1929, declaring the cardinal the official state bird. It was not until 1965 that Illinoisans gave much additional thought to their state bird.

In the June 4, 1965, Daily Illini, published at the University of Illinois in Champaign-Urbana, Eric Wolff wrote:

"A curious bit of Americana can be seen in the custom of having a particular bird and flower designated by state legislatures as 'official.'

"The selection of the species to be so honored is usually not a very difficult process. Economic consideration seems to outweigh other factors.

"For example, the ring-necked pheasant was chosen to be the state bird of South Dakota. Nearly 70,000 non-resident hunters visit the state annually in search of the game bird. They spend over $6 million while they are there.

"Michigan, publicizing its winesap apples, chose the apple blossom as its state flower. Kansas, which grows and ships hundreds of carloads of sunflower seeds to other states each year adopted the sunflower as its own. The Rhode Island Red is the state bird of its namesake.

"Illinois is an exception to this rule. The brilliant red cardinal was selected as the state bird by school children in 1929. The cardinal was one of five species listed on the ballot. Until very recently, not much objection was heard about the students' choice."

Statewide debate was long and although sometimes heated, most of it was in a very reasonable, thoughtful, and sometimes humorous vein. Typical of those who supported the proposed change was John Warren, author of the "Prairie Trails" column in the Moline Daily Dispatch:

"The cardinal is one of the most beloved of all birds — especially to this writer. . . .But I am not prejudiced against changing designation of the Illinois state bird from the cardinal to the purple martin. I am sure such action would not harm the saucy redbird at all, nor make him downcast one whit.

"The cardinal won his place as Illinois' state bird in 1929, in competition against only four other birds. . . .Significantly, the purple martin wasn't on the ballot. Also significantly, a total of 68 other species received write-in votes.

"One point in which Illinois has achieved its customary mediocrity should come to light at this time — the cardinal is not only our official state bird, but it is also the state bird of six other states, Indiana, Kentucky, North Carolina, Ohio, Virginia and West Virginia.

"The purple martin, beautiful and extremely beneficial, is not the official bird of any state.

"Illinois could not go far wrong in changing."

Many who opposed the change did so primarily because of the proposal's commercial aspects. They professed to be disturbed because the change would benefit some part of the economy and implied that this disqualified any of the martin's other merits from consideration.

Comments such as, "It is interesting to note that the Trio Manufacturing Company, of which Wade is president, builds bird houses," were common among reporters discussing my remarks on the floor of the House.

Backers of the proposal were not ashamed of the economic benefits which could accrue to the state and to Griggsville, and some writers saw no reason why they should be. The editor of the Pike County Democrat-Times, in Pittsfield, wrote:

"It may be of interest to remember that virtually every member of the group which framed the United States Constitution benefited financially from the new setup under the Constitution. . . .But does that mean that our founding fathers were merely crass commercialists, or that they were men whose personal interests coincided with the best interests of the country?"

As the debate grew, various organizations marshalled for the fray, but the issue never came to a final vote. Rep. Morris withdrew his proposal, recognizing that the bill was in danger of defeat and that it had already accomplished much of a beneficial nature.

Comment continued for some time afterward. The debate stimulated reams of humorous writing. The Mt. Morris Index introduced as its own authority a "Dr. Asa Featherwaite," a bird expert who claimed to have developed the parrogeon, a cross between a parrot and a pigeon that so improved battlefield communications by delivering messages verbally that it was instrumental in winning World War II.

Mike Royko, then of the Chicago Daily News, announced that downstate Illinois was having too great a say in the naming of a state bird and that the city should be heard from. He proposed the city pigeon, which he considered ideal, saying, "This bumbling slob of a bird is, in many ways, typical of our modern, urban life.

"Take, for example, some of his best-known characteristics.

"A person is easily charmed by the cooing, soothing, pleasant sounds made by the city pigeon.

"So you throw him a few peanuts or breadcrumbs.

"Then he takes off on one of his short flights, directly overhead, and the same person who gave him the goodies will curse and shout: 'Look what the foul creature did to me.'"

The controversy of 1965 provoked a lot of mixed emotions — and a new interest in birds. The intense emotions soon faded from even the most fervent supporters of the two birds, but the genuine widespread interest in birds continued to grow. In retrospect, many who condemned House Bill 1058 most heartily soon recognized the benefits that resulted.

Many echoed the sentiments of Russell Carter, a naturalist of Schenectady, New York, and an Illinoisan by birth. He wrote in 1966 that while he did "have to admit to a certain reticence to go along with the business then afoot to downgrade the cardinal. . . .I do commend the Trio organization for original and significant contributions to the conservation of a valuable asset in our communities across the nation. The voices of the martins and the cardinals too often have been stilled rather than heard in the name of human progress."

THE GREAT STATE BIRD PRINT PROGRAM

Our interest in state birds did not die with the withdrawal of House Bill 1058.

Three years later it surfaced again when the Society launched a program unprecedented in the history of wildlife art. When the State Bird

Purple Martin Junction is a 10-acre parklike setting that includes the Nature House plant, Nature Society offices, 40 martin houses, and a purple train — 34 cars, steam engine and caboose. Fifteen reconditioned cars contain museums and galleries. This very ambitious project was started in 1972 when the route of the Central Illinois Expressway was announced with plans to pass near this site. First displays were open seven seasons but closed in 1983 pending resolution of legal tangles that had stalled construction of the highway.

The purple martin was responsible for both our tourism and wildlife art business. In 1969 we opened the Griggsville Wildlife Art Center with 14 rooms of art objects grouped around a beautiful gallery displaying hundreds of framed antique and contemporary wildlife classics. But on May 9, 1970, just five months after it was opened, the center was struck by lightning and destroyed by fire. Two years later, work was started on the 10-acre complex that became known as Purple Martin Junction.

Print Program was completed another 10 years later, every state owned a set of 22"x28" prints of the 29 species honored as official symbols — with every print bearing the official seal and governor's signature from that state.

The circumstances leading to the program are these:

In 1967, after the discovery of artist Richard Sloan, we had commissioned Sloan to paint a series of 10 very large (40"x30") paintings depicting the life history of the martin.

The series was impressive, to say the least. Consequently, we were inspired to consider a collector print series unlike anything in this century. This series would be the first since Audubon's on a large, standardized format that could be bound into prestige volumes. The interest they would create in birds would be great, we felt, and the very first subject in the series would be the bird responsible for it — the purple martin.

As the series began to develop, so did our involvement in other aspects of wildlife art — antiques, publishing, education, tourism. In 1968, with a growing stream of visitors to Griggsville, we started to develop a plan that would offer them something special to see here.

In late 1969, the Griggsville Wildlife Art Center was opened. In a large central gallery we displayed possibly the world's largest collection of framed antique and contemporary wildlife art — Audubons, Wilsons, Goulds, Selbys, many more. Other rooms contained thousands of art objects — all with bird themes — imported from all around the world.

In early 1970 it burned to the ground.

Lightning struck the Center shortly after 11 a.m. on Saturday, May 9, and traveling on electrical circuits started several scattered fires simultaneously. Fortunately, only five persons were in the building. Those five persons and one piece of furniture got out safely.

Sloan's monumental "life history" series, the first six originals in his collector series, a fortune in antique wildlife prints and art objects did not get out. Everything was lost.

But our tourism and art programs survived. The tourism program eventually resulted in Purple Martin Junction. The art program resulted in not one but three landmark print series — the birds of Richard Sloan, mammals of Richard Timm and flowers of Maryrose Wampler. And among the 50 subjects painted by Sloan were all of the 29 species honored as state birds.

As plates 2, 3 and 4 came into existence — the eastern bluebird, ring-necked pheasant and cardinal are all state birds — we knew something very special was building. We felt it would be very unfortunate if this series went unnoticed by the general public. Acceptance by a limited collector market was not enough.

So we designed the State Bird Program. Each of the 50 states would be given a complete set of these high quality prints. Each would be signed by the appropriate governor and carry that state seal. Each of the participating governors would be given 40 additional prints to present to citizens of his state who had made contributions to wildlife conservation. Ten more would be reserved by the Society for the artist and various museum and educational programs.

It proved an undertaking of gigantic proportions.

The cardinal, for example, is the bird of seven states. That meant each of those governors signed 340 prints (50+40+40+40+40+40+40+40+10). The meadowlark is the bird of six states; the mockingbird, five states; the goldfinch and robin, three states each; the eastern bluebird and black-capped chickadee, two each.

It was a white-glove operation, with all signatures to be personally applied (as opposed to machine-applied). The cooperation we received from the governors and their staffs was outstanding. Even so, the logistics were awesome.

Who would have imagined we could move these quantities of prints from one capital to another and work them into the schedules of the world's busiest executives with as much efficiency as it was done? The fact that the subject was birds helped a very great deal.

To tell the story of the State Bird Program would require a book in itself. Many of the past two decades' leading political names appear on these museum prints — Ronald Reagan, Jimmy Carter, Nelson Rockefeller, George Wallace, Reuben Askew, Dale Bumpers, Cecil Andrus, Gerald Ford, to name a few. Ford was the President who signed prints of the "Bald Eagle," which climaxed the series.

We think future generations will agree the project was worth the time, effort and expense. These 29 prints project the enthusiasm American citizens feel for our great natural heritage — and the signatures and seals of our generation's best known leaders make it official.

In most cases these sets are in the custody of state libraries or conservation departments. To learn which agency displays the collection in your state, you can contact the Nature Society, Griggsville, Illinois 62340.

Chapter 4

The Martin and Mosquito Debate

During the two decades we have been involved in the purple martin program, we have become more and more convinced that martins are effective in mosquito control in a large number of situations. After all this time, there is still very little evidence acceptable to the most rigid scientific minds, but the circumstantial evidence is overwhelming.

Testimonials have always been easy to obtain. These are typical:

Mrs. E. C. Shaver, who had approximately 80 martins in her three houses, wrote, "Before I put up my martin house, the mosquitoes were so bad at our house we couldn't stay outside very much. When I went to work in my garden, the mosquitoes were so bad I couldn't work but a few minutes at a time. Now we hardly ever see a mosquito around our house."

Jim Bland Jr. of the Walnut Ridge, Arkansas, Times Dispatch, wrote, ". . .I guess we have 500 boxes in town and a surprising number of martins. Except in areas where there are lots of trees, most houses have martins. . .We have no mosquitoes. When I ask someone about this, they affirm that they have no mosquitoes, and then we start to wonder if the martins had anything to do with it. Suffice it to say that for the first time in many years, mosquitoes are not now a problem here. . .those who do not attribute the lack of pests to the martins are at a loss to explain the cause of the change."

Mary G. Kendrick of Franklin Manor on the Bay at Churchton, Maryland, wrote, "Through the Franklin Manor Citizens Association, Frank (Kendrick) promoted a purple martin landlord project. By March. . .there were 52 landlords in this neighborhood, 57 martin houses and 682 compartments. . .The purple martins have brought a new dimension of nature lore to our community as we sit unmolested by mosquitoes in the summer evenings watching the martins put on their show of swift and graceful acrobatics."

Those are just samples. Over the years we have accumulated hundreds of testimonials — perhaps thousands — but we are still looking for scientifically acceptable cases. They have been hard to come by.

One case that has figured heavily in the debate is that of Dr. Don Micks

This colony on a lake near Grand Rapids, Michigan was that of the late Raleigh Stotz, who conducted much research there. He was perhaps better known for his Bluebirds and Martins Unlimited program, which he led for the Grand Rapids Audubon Club in the 1960s and '70s. It resulted in considerable expansion of housing for both species in a several-state area.

who, at that time, was a staff member of the Department of Preventive Medicine at the University of Texas in Galveston. The incident happened in 1957 and he did not record any data at the time, but his recollection of the incident is convincing:

"Approximately 10 years ago in late spring," he wrote in 1967, "on Bolivar peninsula in Galveston county, near Gilchrist, Texas, a jeep in which I was riding hit a purple martin. The dead bird was picked up, the stomach removed and the contents of the stomach were taken out for observation. It was relatively simple to determine that the stomach was full of mosquitoes, most of which were identifiable as **Aedes sollicitans**." (This is an extremely pestiferous salt marsh species.) "This was hardly surprising in view of the fact that huge populations of this species were in the area at the time these martins were active. It is emphasized that this was a single observation of a single bird, and no data were recorded. I recall that the stomach was essentially full and that there were few, if any, insects other than mosquitoes present in it."

In a subsequent telephone conversation he estimated the number at 300. Dr. Micks was reluctant to draw any strong conclusions about martins as mosquito-controlling agents on the basis of that one bird, but he commented that he found it "reasonable to presume that the populations of all flying insects would be less in the neighborhoods in which martins colonize."

In 1968, Frank A. Bailey of Westerly, Rhode Island, who at that time had had martins for 16 years, wrote. . ."My place is free of mosquitoes when the purple martins are around. I found one that got hit by a car and cut it open, finding loads of mosquitoes which it had eaten. . ."

The following is a letter which appeared originally in 1972 in the Minneapolis Star:

"To the editor: I used to doubt the bird lovers who asserted purple martins could consume astronomical numbers of mosquitoes. Now I am a believer. Tuesday morning (May 8) I looked out our kitchen window and saw black hordes of mosquitoes clinging to the eaves and fascia of our breezeway. Apparently this was an overnight invasion from a nearby breeding area. As the sun rose they flew away. But as soon as this happened we had an invading army of purple martins.

"I live on the hill east of Moore Lake and we always have purple martins but this invasion was like the Macedonian legions.

"All week the martins swooped and dived and twisted and each night there were fewer mosquitoes. Sunday, May 13, was mop-up day for the martins. They left that night, only a few natives remaining, and the area was clean, there were no mosquitoes.

"I knew the birds were beneficial, but they flew in such numbers and were motivated by such a strong compulsion that the effect was something like that in Hitchcock's movie, 'The Birds.'

"Howard LaPray, Fridley, Minnesota"

(This letter appears to make a strong case for the claim that martins do eat large numbers of mosquitoes. At the very least — even if it turned out that LaPray did not identify the insects correctly — the letter is convincing evidence that martins can get overwhelmingly interested in insects considered by some critics too small to warrant the martin's attention.)

Junius Henderson, in his 1927 often-quoted book, "The Practical Value of Birds," wrote, "It is said that the mosquitoes that disturbed the Lyceum entertainments at Lake Winona, Indiana, disappeared after a large number of purple martins were encouraged to nest in boxes provided for them."

Much more about Winona Lake was written by Col. Isaac Brown in his book, "Birds That Work for Us," published in 1911. He wrote:

"Eleven years ago the grounds surrounding Winsome Winona Lake, Indiana, were infested during the summer season by mosquitoes. I have often seen hundreds of ladies sitting in the Chautauqua Auditorium holding lighted rattans by their faces in order that the smoke might keep the mosquitoes away while they listened to the lectures and music. The officers of the association began casting about for remedies. They sought the man with the crude petroleum who could put it on the stagnant water and destroy mosquitoes by that process. They looked to latter day science for remedies, but while they were looking they were shrewd enough to counsel with some old time Hoosiers and were told that those mosquitoes

The city with the longest history of public efforts to house martins is Greencastle, Pennsylvania, which first attracted them to its Center Square in 1840. The birds abandoned that site for 15 years following the War Between the States, then returned and were popular fixtures until 1963, when they again left for reasons unknown. In 1976, in a good will gesture toward the original "purple martin town," the Nature Society donated six Trio Castles (which, fittingly enough, are trimmed in green) to the city in hopes a change of facilities would change the city's luck. They were photographed by Ken Peiffer of the Waynesboro Record Herald, while city employees Richard Bingaman and Tom Green were erecting the new houses. The other photo, by Dennis Shaw of the Hagerstown, Maryland, Morning Herald, shows one of the old houses that had been abandoned.

were bird food and that they should get more air scavenging birds to Winsome Winona Lake. They erected 10 purple martin homes that year. Every one of them was occupied. Next year they erected more homes, and so on each year until last year they had more than 800 pairs of purple martins flitting through the air above that delightful, blessed spot. The lighted rattans are gone forever. The places that 10 years ago were deserted in the evenings on account of mosquitoes are now Lovers' Lanes."

Most purple martin landlords in the Nature Society feel the martins are effective. For years we surveyed the members each year on various subjects. In a typical year, 85 percent indicated they do feel their martins help control their mosquitoes. The "no" and "undecided" categories each typically recorded 7-8 percent.

These percentages of course varied from year to year as a portion of the membership changed, and various weather factors affected their impressions. In 1975 the "yes" votes were 80 percent, which was about as low as that category ever dipped, but I want to site those responses because that year we recorded some other useful statistics with it.

Yes: 80% (Average nesting pairs of this group: 18.72)
No: 6% (Average nesting pairs: 10.89)
Undecided: 14% (Average nesting pairs: 3.28)

As you will notice, members with large colonies were more definite about the mosquito question.

Most of the "no" votes were concentrated in southern coastal and northern water areas, in particular Florida, Louisiana, Minnesota and Ontario, suggesting that these came from areas of high mosquito concentrations where no one thing can have a very noticeable effect. Other factors could account for some of these answers, too. Some colonies, for example, may adjoin areas of heavy tree cover in which martins do not operate.

In general, our membership is very convinced martins are effective and they accompany their votes with emphatic remarks and exclamation points.

The most serious challenge to the martin's reputation as a mosquito-eater came in 1968, when a Florida entomologist, Dr. Herbert Kale, published a study that concluded the martin's mosquito consumption was insignificant. That study, however, was only a new interpretation of existing information and did not include any original research data.

In brief, Dr. Kale based his conclusion on the beliefs that (1) martins feed during the day and mosquitoes are active at night; (2) martins feed high in the air and mosquitoes stay close to the ground; and (3) two sets of stomach analyses showed very few mosquitoes in them.

In answering that report, I pointed out that some of the most bothersome types of mosquitoes are active both day and night; that

J. Warren Jacobs of Waynesburg, Pennsylvania, built a martin house business that was truly noteworthy until changing times killed it off earlier in this century. His ornate houses graced some of the most famous estates in America. "The Capitol" was one of his most elaborate. It had 101 rooms, 21-ft. hinged pole, shipping weight of 800 pounds, and a cost of $185 in 1928, the last record I have of this house being offered. The size and difficulty of cleaning these houses made them impractical for modern needs, but they made striking contributions to the American landscape.

martins feed actively in early morning and late evening when pest mosquito activity is most intense; that martins are very active at low as well as high levels; and that the two stomach studies were useless for answering this particular question because they were accompanied by no data that showed what foods were available to the sampled birds. In addition, I pointed out that a single martin that had been discovered with 300 mosquitoes in its stomach was being unfairly ignored.

The studies Dr. Kale referred to were those of Prof. F. E. L. Beal in 1918 and Dr. R. F. Johnston in 1967. Let's look at those.

THE BEAL STUDY

In 1918, ornithologist F. E. L. Beal analyzed stomach contents of 205 martins said to have been collected "from February to September throughout the United States and Canada." No data concerning circumstances nor exact locations of the specimens were included in his report — nor any indication these birds had ever had a chance to eat mosquitoes on the day each was killed.

Beal listed the scientific order of each insect type found, with the percentage of total intake represented by each. Hymenoptera topped the chart with 23 present. This order included bees (no worker honeybees were found), wasps, ants, sawflies, gallflies and others.

As far as I know, this is the only martin house designed by Frank Lloyd Wright. It belongs to the Albright-Knox Art Gallery in Buffalo, and in 1976 was placed on long-term loan to the Darwin D. Martin house in Buffalo. It was built in 1904, made of stone, with height of 79 inches and width of 65 inches. It was a gift to the museum from Jacob J. and William F. Brach. At last report, it had not attracted martins, which is not surprising in view of its wide open construction. I suspect Wright was more concerned with creating a design effect with this house than with actually attracting martins.

But Diptera, which includes mosquitoes, gnats and flies, provided 16 percent. These were found in 50 stomachs and were the sole contents of seven. Interestingly, Beal found many daddy long legs among the Diptera.

Coleoptera provided 12.5 percent. This included beetles and weevils, and Beal reported that "many were small dung beetles which hover over cow droppings in the early evening and so are easily captured by martins."

In his paper, Kale stated that "martins fly anywhere from 100 or 200 feet above the ground." If this were correct, how did Beal's martins gather such large harvests of daddy long legs and dung beetles?

There's much more of interest in the Beal report. It is a very useful study, but not for the purpose of proving how many mosquitoes are — or are not — eaten by martins.

THE JOHNSTON STUDY

Thirty-four martins were captured near Lawrence, Kansas during 1959, 1960 and 1961 by ornithologist Richard F. Johnston of the University of Kansas. These birds were taken during April, May, June and August for the purpose of determining variation of food consumed by martins during

Tony Cico of Point Harbor, North Carolina, built this 142-room house overlooking Albemarle Sound in 1972 and dubbed it "Serenity Hi-Rise." He spent 1,200 hours designing and building the 238-pound structure. It has guard rails, ventilation holes, drainage system, revolving roof-top sun deck, and styling which he described as "Tel Aviv Modern." It also has a remotely controlled doorbell which is used to discourage starlings and sparrows.

these seasons. The Johnston study was conducted in a thoroughly scientific manner and included both qualitative and quantitative analyses of the stomach contents. Johnston detailed his experiments and findings in "Ibis", an ornithological journal, in 1967.

Coleoptera, chiefly the various beetles, showed the highest percentage of occurrence during each of the four months. Highest percentages were in April and May.

Diptera, including flies, mosquitoes, gnats and daddy long legs, occurred with the next greatest frequency, again with April and May the most productive months. Of the Dipteran food, Culcinae (mosquitoes) occurred as 3 percent of the insects taken in April. Johnston's paper does not specifically state the number of mosquitoes found nor the number of stomachs in which these occurred.

Johnston found many species of insects ranging in size from the minute gnats to the relatively giant grasshoppers, and offered conclusive proof that martins are catholic in their taste for insect food. But he did not prove that mosquitoes are an insignificant part of that diet — nor did he suggest this.

This study, too, was not accompanied by data on the food that was most readily available in the areas in which these martins were killed during the times in which they were killed.

A curious twist occurred in 1983, almost 20 years after I had started to use the claim that a purple martin can eat 2,000 mosquitoes a day — I discovered that another martin booster had originated the same statement in the 1920s.

Joseph H. Dodson of Kankakee, Illinois, began to promote songbirds

Neither traffic noise, exhaust fumes, flashing lights nor exposure to wind and rain can discourage a martin from its chosen nest site. This one nested in front of the green light of a traffic signal and was photographed by the Houston Chronicle. The city obligingly turned off the light and erected a temporary substitute set of signals, but probably would not have needed to. Another pair which nested in a green signal in Wichita Falls ignored the blinking light throughout the season.

very early in this century and by the 1920s was making and selling a wide range of birdhouses, bird feeders and accessories, and traveling widely, lecturing on the value of birds.

Although his houses continued to be sold as late as the early 1950s, the business had faded from prominence. I had no recollection of ever having seen either his literature or advertising, although it is possible I had been exposed to Dodson literature as a child in school.

In the 1920s he first began to claim that a martin can eat 2,000 mosquitoes a day and said it was based on the analysis of an actual stomach. Dodson said one of his martins had been accidentally killed and he had had the stomach analyzed by "a state university."

Upon discovering the statement on which his claim was based, we set out in 1983 to try to track down more information. In the archives of the Kankakee Historical Museum we did find considerable material on Dodson, but nothing that shed any light on a scientific base for his 2,000 mosquito claim.

Our conviction about martins is stronger than ever, but our search for scientifically acceptable proof must go on.

THE HONEYBEE HASSLE

Another type of challenge to the martin's reputation was not so difficult to handle. It came from the Houston area in the spring of 1966 when the martin was accused of eating honeybees in great numbers. Joe C. Pouncey, treasurer of the Harris County Beekeepers Association, claimed martins were a menace to bees and all houses should be torn down.

Allison Sanders of the Houston Chronicle relayed Pouncey's sentiments to the public in the April 29, 1966, issue in an editorial entitled, "Bee-Ware the Martin." Sanders wrote:

"There are at least two sides to every question and the truth in this cliche is proved in a letter from Joe C. Pouncey, security officer at the San Jacinto Bank of Pasadena and treasurer of the Harris County Beekeepers Association.

"Until Pouncey's letter arrived I had felt, as most people probably do, that purple martins are as sacrosanct as motherhood and the flag — they eat mosquitoes, so who could be against them?

Pouncey and the other beekeepers are, to name several.

"'Who in the world sponsored this hoax of purple martins eating mosquitoes?' Pouncey demands. 'They really are the most predaceous enemy the honeybee has. Why would a martin go to the trouble of hunting mosquitoes when, with no effort at all, he can soar above the approach to a colony of honeybees and pick off the workers coming in so loaded with honey that they can't even take evasive action?

"'Martins feed during the day, while the mosquitoes are safely hidden in the grass and weeds. About the time the mosquitoes come out in the late evening the martins are full of honeybees and heading to their nice apartment complexes, built by unthinking humans who don't realize the importance of the honeybee.'

"If martins and mosquitoes and honeybees wore hats," concluded Sanders, "like in TV westerns, it wouldn't be so hard to tell the bad guys from the good guys."

The Houston Post also published Pouncey's comments, and several other newspapers and radio commentators also noticed the comments and relayed them to the public, sometimes accompanied with an unspoken, but obvious, "Aha!"

Not everyone agreed with Pouncey, however.

John James Audubon would not have agreed. He flatly declared, "These birds seldom seize the honeybee." Many more recent observers wouldn't agree, either. The Chronicle and Post were deluged with letters in the martin's defense.

The real culprit is the eastern kingbird, or "bee martin," which does have an appetite for honeybees. But it is a member of the flycatcher family, not even a swallow.

The kingbird in color and general configuration (having almost black wings, tail and upper part, and with a fan-shaped tail) can, by the unacquainted, be easily mistaken for the purple martin, particularly the female of the species. This bird may well be the enemy of beekeepers, but you can be sure it is the friend of every farmer, for it is the undaunted foe of crows, hawks and many other large predatory birds.

Pete Jury of Houston, who has a beehive in his yard, wrote that he resented the articles condemning martins. "Other people with bees and purple martin houses have never seen the purple martin catch a bee. . ."

Jim Tom House of Houston referred to Bulletin 179, and pointed out that the Beal study said, "To accusations that martins destroy honeybees, he had a definite answer that in only five of 200 stomachs did honeybees appear, and every one of them was a drone."

Joe F. Combs reported in his "Farm Corner" column in the Beaumont Enterprise the experience of B. B. Horn of Vidor, Texas, who had a swarm of bees actually using one of the gourds used by martins on his place. Horn's observations were among the most interesting to surface during that little controversy:

"'There is a male purple martin that belongs in a 25-compartment house about 50 feet away (from the bees) that has the habit of crawling into and resting or sleeping in the gourd next to the one the bees have taken over. I have been watching him now for five days. When he goes into the gourd several bees go over to where he sits with his head out the hole.

"'When the bees come near he just shakes his head. The bees don't bother him, and he doesn't bother the bees. So if anyone believes purple martins eat honeybees, they are wrong, and I have the proof right here at my place. . .'"

We have continued to receive reports over the years from beekeepers who also house martins, but I can't remember a single report from a beekeeper who had a serious loss to martins.

A typical case is that of Richard Vansandt, the St. Augustine gentleman who has 100 martins on his 47-acre tract. He also has 30 beehives and is president of the Northeast Florida Beekeepers Association.

While purple martins may occasionally take a drone, the bird known as the "bee martin" is actually the eastern kingbird, a member of the flycatcher family.

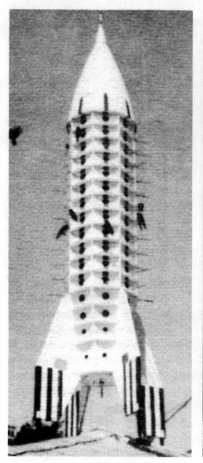

One of the more intriguing designs is this rocket house with 128 compartments at the home of Richard A. Buttke in Milwaukee. It's made of fir plywood, aluminum nose cone, steel-covered fins, and supported by four steel tubes. According to Buttke, it's easy to clean, too. Before anyone undertakes a design this large or complex, he should be certain that an easy maintenance system is designed into it.

The late Charlie Butler of Arkansas City, Kansas, then vice president of the NAPPPMBA, replaced this windmill house with five of the new Trio aluminum houses in 1964. Although this was done with some hesitancy, Butler soon became one of the leading boosters for the new type of housing. He filled virtually all of the 60 new compartments and the ease of management allowed him to produce more young martins than in any previous year.

This is the colony of Tom Beasley of Oakland City, Indiana. During the 15 years prior to his death in 1984, Beasley conducted much research on martins, especially on sparrow control.

This is part of the colony of Dimitry Morvant of New Orleans, who participated in a televised debate on the martin's effectiveness as a mosquito-eater in 1968. He subsequently became known as "the purple martin's best friend in New Orleans." Morvant invited skeptics to visit his home both before and after the martins departed each year, and notice the difference.

The late Reuben Chandler and Mrs. Chandler of Mackenzie, Tennessee built up one of the world's largest colonies in this spectacular array of homemade aluminum houses. Approximately 1,000 martins leave there each year.

George Finey needed 38 days to build this 620-room house near Winnfield, Louisiana. It's 8' long, 4' wide, 8.5' tall, cost $530 to build, and requires two gallons of paint to cover it one time. At last report it was home to around 200 martins.

This house, similar in style to those popularized around the turn of the century by J. Warren Jacobs, is in the center of Somerset, Pennsylvania, another town that is well known for its martin interest. I don't know whether the clock works.

Section B

The Purple Martin Story

SY?

Let's make sure we are speaking the same language

Let's make sure we are talking the same language.

Most popular literature, including our own Nature Society News, refers to martins in their first nesting season as "first-year birds" and older birds as "mature" or "adult" birds.

Scientific writings, however, refer to birds in their first nesting season as "second year" (SY) birds and older birds as "after second year" (ASY) birds.

In this book I will use the scientific terms. At first glance this may cause a little confusion among a majority of martin enthusiasts who use the "first-year" and "adult" designations, but there are two good reasons for the change:

First, although this isn't a scientific treatise, I will be quoting some scientific studies, and the book must use one consistent set of terms that will apply to both scientific and popular writings.

Second, the scientific terms are accurate. "First-year" nesters are actually in their second calendar year of life, so it is entirely appropriate they be referred to as "second-year."

There's another good reason, too. "SY" and "ASY" take up less space than "first-year" and "adult" so once we all get used to using them we can move along more quickly and maybe take two pages off the length of this book.

ASY?

Chapter 5

Getting Acquainted

Purple martins are the largest of the swallows.

Swallows have long, pointed wings and most have notched or deeply forked tails. All are strong, elegant fliers and all depend mainly — some entirely — on catching their food on the wing. Legs are short and used for perching. Bills are short and wide and used for scooping insects from the air. All are social species, tending to nest in colonies, although a couple of species prefer to scatter in loose colonies. All are cavity-nesters.

Swallows are among the most popular of families. Among the dozen or so species in North America are cliff swallows, the famous birds of Capistrano that build bottle-shaped mud cavities on the walls of buildings and sides of cliffs; the very similar cave swallows that nest in limestone caves in parts of New Mexico and Texas; barn swallows, the colorful and spectacular fliers that plaster their nesting cups to the rafters of farm buildings; bank and rough-winged swallows, that burrow into steep banks and the walls of gravel pits; tree and violet-green swallows, that like to nest in single-cavity birdhouses in the open countryside; and purple martins.

Among other members of their family, the two-ounce, broad-shouldered, all-black purple martin looks like a giant. Mature male martins are the only swallows with dark plumage over the entire body. Their voice is very different from that of any other swallow. And there is at least one other, very important difference.

Martins are the only swallow species that will nest in large numbers in multi-compartment birdhouses. They show a marked preference for nesting near human activity, and this has given them a unique status in all of the bird world. They are aptly termed "semi-domesticated" and purple martins and humans have a relationship that is very beneficial to both parties.

In this chapter I will describe the physical characteristics of martins, their nests and eggs. Most information on behavior, however, will be included in the next chapter, which deals in great detail with the life cycle.

Information on where martins can be attracted will be included in the

Cliff swallow at nests, by Karl Maslowski.

Barn swallow at nest, by Gary Seib. (This photo is included in Canada's National Collection of Nature Photographs in the National Museum in Ottawa.)

chapter on range, where I will also discuss types of terrain, elevations, ground cover and other factors. This will lead up to chapter 10, in which I will present recommendations on how to attract, manage and build a healthy colony.

SIZE

A mature purple martin is 7-1/2 inches long and weighs 1-1/2 to 2 ounces. A female may appear slightly smaller than a male, but that's probably due to more subdued coloration. There is no significant difference in weight.

This weight range is less than listed in some previous writings, including my own on the subject. Basing my estimate on some earlier references, I had considered 3-1/2 to 4 ounces to be typical, but extensive testing in the 1970s clearly established the weight at much less than that.

Kathy Klimkiewicz and Paul Jung, the research team that has been banding and studying martins for more than 10 years in the Washington, D.C. area, weighed several hundred adults and reported, "Males range from 46.3 to 57.9 grams and females from 44.8 to 59.0 grams. Combined

The purple martin's family in North America includes eight other swallows — barn, bank, cliff, cave, tree, violet-green and northern rough-winged swallows, plus gray-breasted martins (found only in Mexico, Central and South America). The only ones that normally colonize around human homes, however, are the barn swallow, cliff swallow (as of Capistrano) and tree swallow (and, in the far west, the violet-green). Only one can normally be attracted in large numbers to multiple-compartment birdhouses — the purple martin.

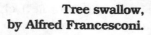

Tree swallow, by Alfred Francesconi.

adults range from 44.8 to 59.0 grams with an average of 51.0 grams. There is no significant difference between males and females or between SY (second-year) and ASY (after-second-year) birds."

An ounce equals 28.3 grams, so that means the average adult martin weighs slightly less than two ounces.

Wings, which typically span 15 inches, and the mildly forked tail, are both proportionately broader than those of most swallows. More than other swallows, martins spend time on the wing, gliding and soaring apparently just for the enjoyment of it.

I'm sure some of what appears to be casual flight is not, however. Martins are sometimes feeding when they appear to be drifting aimlessly.

Visually, martins appear in a general size range with starlings, robins, cardinals, catbirds and other medium-sized backyard birds — bigger than sparrows, smaller than blue jays.

PLUMAGE

Most often, martins appear only as rather ordinary black and gray birds — not very exciting to the uninitiated. But when sunlight strikes them, particularly the older males, the black areas become brilliant iridescent purple, and their name suddenly becomes very appropriate.

Martins breed during the first nesting season after their first winter migration, but they do not achieve adult plumage until they molt during their second winter. Until that time both sexes pretty closely resemble an adult female, and this often causes confusion in identification.

Mature males are easy to recognize — they're the all-black ones — but even veteran observers have trouble distinguishing among mature females and second-year males and females. They usually can be identified, however, if you want to strongly enough. One key may be that males of all ages are darker on the top of the head than females of all ages.

Here are some distinguishing characteristics:

ASY males: Completely blue-black.

ASY females: Blue-black on top of head and back. Gray on chin, breast and abdomen.

SY males: Similar to ASY females except darker on the head and back and lighter on the underparts. Gray on the forehead. Often have a few dark feathers showing on the breast.

SY females: Similar to ASY females, but slightly paler both above and below.

These differences are very subtle, and even veteran observers sometimes have difficulty identifying ages and sexes with 100 percent certainty.

As I will discuss later in the life cycle ("timetable") chapter, SYs usually mate with SYs, and ASYs usually mate with ASYs, so this can be used in getting a general idea of how many of each age group are nesting in your colony. Pairs which appear to be both females are generally both SYs; pairs which have an all-black male are usually both ASYs.

Molt starts in late summer, stops during migration, then resumes at the winter roost, where most plumage change occurs.

Some species drop so many flight feathers at once during molt they cannot fly until replacement feathers grow in. Not so with martins. This species, which must always be able to fly in order to survive, sheds and replaces feathers gradually, and usually drops matched pairs — one on each side — so that flight balance is not affected.

As in most species, albinism does occur. Pure albinos are rare, but partial albinism is rather common. Most colonies are without even partial albinos, but the occurrence of one or even two partials in a colony is not particularly unusual. Some persons have recorded the life spans of partial albinos simply because they were so easy to identify from year to year. I can recall a few cases of partial albinos being reported in colonies for six to eight years before disappearing.

Complete albinos, however, are very unusual, and the occurrence of two in the same nest is alleged to have astronomical statistical odds against it. But we have had two such reports.

In 1971, the Raymond Smiths of Dodge City, Kansas, discovered two pure albinos in the same nest of four young — an extremely rare occurrence. The parents apparently fed the albinos with the same dedication as their normal young, but both experienced problems after fledging. The first to fledge was driven to exhaustion by older birds and died. The second also was grounded but was rescued and fed by the Smiths and their neighbors, the Raymond Reichenborns. This appears to have been a case in which the albinos were not accepted by the colony, but was this actually the case or were these young simply experiencing the harassment from old birds that all fledglings receive and were among that percentage that don't survive it? Photo is by the Dodge City Daily Globe.

In 1977, Bill Lynn, science teacher of Atchison, Kansas, Junior High discovered two complete albinos in a nest of four.

During the 1971 season, J. P. Dixon of West Point, Virginia, found two albinos also in a nest of four. They eventually disappeared and he suspected they were driven out by the other birds in the colony. During another season he watched a neighbor's colony drive out an albino that had fledged there.

While albinos may sometimes be ostracized by others in their colony, it is by no means universal. We have had a number of reports of albinos functioning normally in colonies.

SONG

The first person to describe a bird song as a "chirp" was probably a martin enthusiast, because some of their sounds come closer to being "chirps" than any bird song I can think of. Quite often you may read of the martin song described as a "liquid, rolling chirrup," but the full range is much more complex than that.

Dr. John William Hardy, long-time student of martins and curator of birds at the Florida State Museum in Gainesville, has published a long-play 33 rpm record, "Sounds of Purple Martins." In one of the narrative sections, he comments:

The purple martin "has a more elaborate language than most birds, and displays a marvelous range of expressiveness, from soft conversational gurglings through emphatic and excited chortlings. . .happy sounds and sad sounds. . .and piercing sounds of apparent joy, anger and fear."

In a section on "martinese," he shows a clear difference between the male and female residence possession songs. The female counterpart is more delicate and subdued, and only hints at the ratcheting sound that is the male's trademark.

After demonstrating the insistent alarm notes used when they are frightened, and mentioning the alarm squawk used when they attack something, he lumped most other sounds into a repertoire of "chirps and gurgles." He calls these "social convention sounds," used in miscellaneous group activities and often accompanied by wings being flipped upward.

In an earlier study, "Behavior of the Purple Martin," published in the Wilson Bulletin in 1962, Dr. Hardy and Dr. Richard F. Johnston wrote, "The song of the male martin is a complex series of distinct notes running three or four seconds in time. An initial series of notes, most frequently just two (phonetically, 'churr'), is followed by two notes ('sweet') of different quality, and is rounded off by a warbled set of heavy, guttural, but musical clicks. The song may be given in aggressive interchanges, in the greeting of a mate on its return, or in proclamation of territoriality... apparently the same set of sounds has different meanings when used with different postural attitudes and in different social situations. . ."

Hardy and Johnston described the alarm notes, such as when used when frightened by a predator, as "kiv-kiv, kiv kiv keer, keer keer keer, kiv keer keer. Kiv is uninflected; keer has a downward inflection. The initial notes kiv-kiv may actually be the important notes of stress and alarm; the notes keer, etc. are given while the birds are in flight or engaged in mobbing the agent of alarm."

Finally, they described the note of high intensity alarm as "Zwrack!" That's a note many martin enthusiasts will identify with immediately, since many have been "dive-bombed" by one or more individuals in a colony. (There's been much discussion over the years whether these strafing attacks are playful or aggressive; my guess is that they are almost always aggressive, and done because of an imagined threat to the bird's house or young.)

Hardy and Johnston said they noticed only minor differences between sounds of males and females, and between mature and immature birds. "Most of the notes of females are slightly muffled counterparts of the notes of males. . ." they wrote, and ". . .the song of many first-year males is shorter than songs of most adults, lacking so full a series of guttural clicks in the terminal part."

Gary Berger of Houston noticed the one distinctive type of male song mentioned above by Hardy and Johnston, but described it a bit differently. In 1973 he wrote, "I have two or three young males with a few black feathers on their chests, and I am almost completely sure these are first-year males. . .it has come to my attention that only the male of the species can make the sound that resembles a stick-on-a-picket fence. . .I have seen the black males and the first-year males (ones with the few black feathers) make this sound, but I have never seen or heard a "sure" female (one with a black mate) make this sound."

NIGHT FLIGHT

While martins are not nocturnal in the sense they regularly fly and feed at night, they are occasionally in the air at different times of the night, and explanations for all cases are not clear.

One type of night-time singing is common, however, and pretty well defined. This is the "dawn song," or singing done by males just before dawn during certain times in the nesting cycle. Eugene S. Morton of Severna Park, Maryland, describes it this way: ". . .males only leave the colony at about 4:15-5:15 a.m. from early May through late June. They fly to an elevation of about 800-1,000 feet (a guesstimate) and dawn sing. The dawn song is a continuous and very syncopated series of staccato notes sounding like 'chip, chip, chiree, chirp' repeated over and over. This is quite unlike the courtship song with the raspy end given during the day at the colony.

"The males that deliver this dawn song, and not all the breeding males dawn sing every day, are already mated and may already have small young. No known function can be as yet ascribed to this behavior. Guesses are that martins do defend feeding territories and the song functions to keep others away, or that males still try to attract females after pairing."

Mrs. S. E. Warford of Breckenridge, Texas, noticed what appeared to be a correlation between dawn singing and the laying of first eggs and hatching of first young. Her observations appear to indicate the function of the song is something as simple as happiness. She wrote:

"I eagerly wait and listen. . .for the day or the night the first egg is laid. For the last three years I have known exactly when it was.

"I am an early riser and near 4:30 or 5 a.m. the day of the first egg the male bird sits on the highest perch he can find in our yard. . .This dear potential father sings his heart out with happiness.

"It is not the regular call or warble; it is really a prolonged song. I always tell my husband we will have a martin egg today. Sure enough I lower the box later in the day and there is the lovely little white egg.

"The same thing happens when the first baby is hatched. . .The singing goes on for some time, always before daylight, and is carried on by each prospective father when the first eggs and first babies come. I'm very anxious for some other purple martin landlords to hear and verify my discoveries. . ."

Bobby and Lorraine Rose of Nashville, North Carolina recently wrote, "We can also confirm that martins do fly at night. One morning in the middle of May my husband got up to turn out the dog. It was 4 a.m. and a full moon. He heard commotion in the yard, thought it was coming from our martin houses. Upon investigating, he found out that chirping and twittering was coming from the sky. . .

"Our martins were asleep and quiet. My husband sat out in the yard until daybreak (about 5:30 a.m.) when our martins came out of their houses and perched on top. Upon seeing our martins, three came down from the sky, landed and stayed. Rest of the flock, circling in air, moved north."

Do all the expectant fathers in a neighborhood gather in the pre-dawn darkness to share anxieties? What is the exact function of this pre-dawn song that seems to be practiced by only a select few to the complete indifference of the remainder of their colony?

FLIGHT CAPABILITIES

Martins are widely renowned for their flying prowess, being among the most graceful and efficient of aerial feeders. But how fast do they actually fly?

I don't know the top speed of which a martin is capable, but it is safe to say they do not approach the 100-plus miles per hour of some swifts, or the 150-200 miles per hour of a falcon plunging earthward to knock its prey from the sky.

In 1963 and 1964 Gary Schnell used Doppler radar to record the flight speeds of 169 purple martins flying near their colony on a windless day. Top speed was 41 miles per hour. For the group, speeds ranged from 5-41 mph, with a mean of 21.7.

Martins have rather dependable homing tendencies during the nesting period. When released far away from home, most of them will get home, but they apparently are not very efficient at getting there.

A series of studies made at the University of Michigan Biological Station during the years of 1958, 1959, 1960 and 1962 by William Southern, Douglas Lancaster and Larry L. Wolf shed a lot of light on their homing tendencies. During those years they captured 108 nesting martins from houses in Cheboygan County, in northern Michigan, and transported them to locations from a few miles to a few hundred miles away before releasing. The locations were scattered in eight directions from the home colony.

Depending on distances, the return rate varied from 66.7 to 100 percent. For the group as a whole, 79.8 percent returned — four out of five. Return rate declined as distances increased, but even at the maximum distance of 594 miles, two-thirds of the birds returned.

Average speed in getting back to the colony ranged to a high of 27.37 mph, but that speed decreased as distance increased, and the average for the entire group was only 7.24 miles per hour.

They did not notice much difference in success rates between male and female birds or between adult and subadult (SY) birds. But of 12 juveniles released at distances up to 250 miles, only two returned, and those two were released within sight of the colony. Apparently some important learning does occur during the first year of life.

Southern and the other researchers did not learn much about how the martin navigates. There was not much evidence to show whether it uses landmarks, solar references, magnetic influences, or other factors. Land-marks did seem to be at least a partial factor.

Each bird was observed on release, and most but not all circled the release site for awhile before departing in the general direction of the home colony. Southern didn't notice much difference in the return rates or speeds between those that circled and those that didn't.

He also didn't notice much difference between those released on sunny days and those on overcast days. Although solar navigation may be used, there wasn't much evidence of it in these studies.

More about the cross-country navigation of martins will be included in my discussion of migration in chapter 6. For the moment, suffice it to mention that these speeds suggest a rather uncertain or lackadaisical overland pace, even when obviously anxious to reach their homes and young. Even though birds in flocks tend to fly with more purpose, confidence and speed than individuals, this does not sound like the flight habits of a species that would fly 600 miles at a crack over open water when it could hop from island to island or migrate casually up the Mexican coast.

Nevertheless, there is a possibility that some martins do just that — fly 600 miles from Yucatan to Louisiana — each spring, and we'll talk about that in chapter 6.

OTHER SEX DIFFERENCES

Mature (ASY) birds are apparently a bit more effective as parents than second-year (SY) nesters. In a mid-1970s study of 29 nesting pairs, published in the Sept.-Oct., 1975, Inland Bird Banding News, Gary Paul Saner of Arlington, Texas, noted the mature pairs averaged one-half egg more per clutch, but noticed no differences in parenting skills. Success in fledging was the same.

In their study of a much larger number of pairs, however, Klimkiewicz and Jung did find differences. In 1976, Kathy wrote, "SY birds, both male and female do not nest as successfully as ASY birds."

In a report published in 1977 in North American Bird Bander, they wrote, "Our study has shown that. . .SY females lay fewer eggs than ASYs; SY adults occasionally do not feed frequently enough to maintain the normal growth pattern of the young; SY adults often build poorly constructed nests with little or no mud; overall nest success is lower in SY adults. . ."

Over the years at Purple Martin Junction, we have gained the very distinct impression that SY birds are not as successful. Later nests — of which a large percentage are by young pairs — are on the average more poorly made, have fewer eggs, produce fewer successful young, and more often fail completely.

Our records are not complete enough, however, to allow us to say this is clearly the result of poorer parenting or more stressful conditions later in the nesting season when SY birds nest. Perhaps higher average temperatures have an effect; perhaps nest-robbing activities and harassment by sparrows and starlings is more severe; numerous other environmental factors could be involved. Maybe older birds would do just as poorly if they nested that late on the average. But I doubt it.

I believe that parenting instincts in SY birds are not as firmly developed as in ASY birds, and it's as simple as that.

EGGS

Martin eggs are white, ovate, and typically weigh around four grams. They are easy to distinguish from starling and house sparrow eggs, the only other kinds most landlords are apt to find in their houses. Starling eggs are a very pale blue-green, while sparrow eggs are speckled with brown.

J. Warren Jacobs, in 1903, reported he had weighed 65 fresh martin eggs and found their weight range from 3.4 to 4.6 grams, with an average of 4.1 grams. In four sets, which he weighed as they were laid, the first was always the lightest, with each succeeding egg weighing a little more than the one before it.

Most clutches range from 4-6 eggs.

Jacobs also reported on a study of 84 clutches in the Ann Arbor area. He found seven eggs in one percent of the nests; six eggs in 19 percent; five eggs in 54 percent; four eggs in 25 percent; and three eggs in one percent — an average overall of 4.9 per nest.

Otto Widmann in 1922 reported approximately the same breakdown in 45 nests he studied in Missouri, and he made a couple of interesting observations: "In second sets (those laid after a first clutch is destroyed) I have never found any number other than four. All four-egg clutches were either second sets or were laid by the mate of a first-year (SY) male, presumably a first-year (SY) female."

These averages probably agree pretty closely with those here at the Junction. We have noticed that six-egg clutches are more common during seasons in which nesting starts at a normal early time; much less common during later than average seasons.

Ten eggs seems to be the largest reported in a single nest. In 1972 Mr. and Mrs. J. A. Miller of Cleburne, Texas reported 10 eggs in one nest and eight in another. In 1974 James Bumpous of LaCenter, Kentucky, reported a 10-egg clutch, and added that eight of them apparently survived.

Were these record clutches, or the works of more than one female in each case? In the 1977 season Elsa M. Hay of Des Moines found 10 eggs in one nest, but knew they were definitely the work of two females. The second female had started laying in a nest abandoned by another. Ms. Hay culled five eggs — four of which she knew to be bad — and reported that four of the remaining five eventually hatched and fledged.

During the 1978 season, the Reuben Chandlers of McKenzie, Tennessee, found nine young in one nest. Because this house was a single-compartment unit it was impossible for young from another nest to have crawled into it.

In the 1982 season, Joe Grzeskowiak of Hampton, Virginia, reported nine young in one nest, and eight of them fledged.

In 1984, Tom Dellinger of Duncanville, Texas, recorded two 9-egg clutches.

In all of these cases the possibility remains that each is the work of two females, but I suspect some or all of them are just what they appear to be — the rare exceptions that crop up in nature.

For sheer productivity, probably few rival the work of the seven pairs that nested in the colony of Mrs. R. M. Dickerson of Courtland, Virginia in 1978. She found 54 eggs in the seven nests (average of almost eight per nest) and 43 of them eventually hatched. That's an average of slightly more than six per nest.

NESTS

Martins typically nest in a cavity of at least 6"x6"x6", a size which has proved quite adequate and which serves as the standard for modern housing. Some feel a six-inch cavity should be too small for a 7-1/2 inch bird, but that idea is deceptive. Martins can nest successfully even in a five-inch cavity, but the six-inch cavity allows more adequate space for development of five- and six-egg broods. Overall plumage dimension is rarely a factor.

This question is put in clearer perspective by noting the number of adult martins that can pack themselves into a six-inch cube during cold weather. We have had many reports of 12-15 birds packed into a single room, and we have had 15 in a single compartment on at least one occasion in our own colony at the Junction.

We have had several reliable reports of 18-23 martins packed into a single 6"x6"x6" compartment; in 1983 Edward Kingsley of Brookport, Illinois, reported 24 in one compartment; and also in 1983 Kathleen

Use of mud varies widely, both in amount, type of material, and type of construction. Some construct a wall behind the door; some build right out through the door opening; some use little or none. Some, usually SY birds, just scatter mud about randomly without any apparent construction in mind.

Here is a variety of nests that use little or no mud. Nest composition varies from area to area depending on what is available. Strips of cornstalk are heavily used in Purple Martin Junction nests, but so are apple twigs and several types of heavy straw and weed stems.

Coleman of Milford, Virginia, discovered 29 — that's the most we've heard of in a six-inch cube, although we've had a report of 39 exiting a single very large gourd after a cold snap.

Obviously, the actual space needed for a martin to function effectively is not very great.

A typical nest consists of a pad of sticks, grass or other fibrous materials, usually no more than one inch deep, with only a slight depression in the center or toward the back of the cavity. Mud can nearly always be found on the front edge of the nest but its use varies widely from mere traces to extensive mud dikes that nearly close the entrance holes.

This mud barrier is presumed to provide protection against weather, predators, or both, but we don't know why some martins build them and others don't. Quite often mud barriers will be common in certain parts of the Junction colony grounds and not in others. Sometimes they occur only on the sides of houses which face the same direction, but that is not necessarily the direction from which prevailing winds blow.

Whatever the motivation, these barriers obviously do provide some protection, particularly from smaller nest-robbing predators. Larger predators like owls can shove them aside and snakes can slither right over them, however.

Nests show a wide range of craftsmanship. They range from crude mixtures of large sticks and miscellaneous trash to a small percentage that are finely crafted of grasses and other fine fibers. Older birds usually are responsible for the neater, better crafted ones. Regardless of craftsmanship, nearly all nests are lined with small green leaves; at the Junction these are always apple leaves picked in the nearby orchard.

Function of these leaves may be as a coolant or as a natural parasiticide. The coolant theory seems inadequate since martins start using the leaves early in the season while days are still cool or at least comfortable.

The parasiticide theory seems more likely since these decaying leaves give off very small amounts of hydrocyanic acid (HCN) and this is thought to be effective in discouraging nest parasites.

Whatever the purpose, these leaves show up as soon as a nest is completed, and usually continue to appear until the eggs hatch.

The main pad of the nest itself is usually made of sticks and grasses, but a very wide range of materials has been reported. Here are some samples:

J. Paul Perron of St. Jean, Quebec, found a nest with a base of 102 steel nails, each 2-1/2" in length and all obviously new when they had been collected. On top of this was a mat of string, leaves and paper debris.

We don't have many reports of nails, but many listing aluminum can pull tabs. William H. Murphy of Louisville found 98 pull tabs mixed into a nest. Erhard Buntrock photographed a nest from which dozens of tabs had been extracted.

Mr. and Mrs. Hal Wilmarth of Evansville, Indiana, have two 20-room houses. Pull tabs are very common in one but not at all in the other. In the one house, they find "8 to 10 rings in each nest, the same box each year."

Among the array of items landlords have reported to us over the years are popsicle sticks, tinfoil, match covers, gum wrappers, plastic trash, string ties, dryer lint, Spanish moss, shredded cyprus mulch, and "just about anything they can carry."

Not everything they carry home is trash. Louis H. Foell of Louisville found a dollar bill in one nest, neatly folded down to a 1-1/2" square.

But the prize goes to Mrs. Glen Tracy of Wellington, Kansas, who found a very good diamond under her martin house. She reported her birds normally pick up anything bright and shiny, including lots of aluminum cuttings from a nearby plant, plus pieces of glass and foil. She is used to cleaning up such trash from beneath the houses and almost threw this item away before she realized what it was.

Broken glass is a fairly common item in nests, and is a very common item fed to young birds as grit.

Straw is popular. Lonnie Campbell of Sapulpa, Oklahoma, reported his martins love oat straw, and he has watched his martins pick up straws, one at a time, until "they have such a mouthful one would think they couldn't carry it."

Carolina H. Young of Bowie, Maryland, put out a huge ball of cat hair brushings and it was gone in an hour. So the next morning she put out more and "the martins came from all directions and it was gone before I reached the patio."

That willingness to accept artificial supplies of materials is something you can use to your advantage in attracting and building a colony, and I will discuss that in more detail in chapter 10.

LIFE SPAN

Most martins live only a few years. Of those that survive their first year, I believe a majority live only 2-4 seasons. Although many of the hardier birds return to colonies for 6-8 years, individuals that live longer than that in the wild are rare exceptions.

Some martins have lived as house pets for longer periods. One that comes to mind is a bird rescued by Rose Minda of Avella, Pennsylvania, during the destruction of Hurricane Agnes in 1972. This bird would not return to the wild when the time came so she elected to keep it as a house pet. When I last heard of it in 1981, this martin was nine years old and still quite healthy.

Oldest martin of which we have an official record is one that carried U.S. band number B-261331. This bird was banded July 1, 1933 by Lawrence E. Hunter of Dallas City, Illinois. It was found dead under a martin house at Dallas City by biologist George C. Arthur in the spring of 1947 — 13 years and 10 months later.

Chapter 6

The Purple Martin Timetable

Introductory remarks

This lengthy chapter covers everything about purple martins that relates to the calendar, and that's a lot. No other species of wildlife is so linked to the calendar in the minds of its admirers.

Nearly all martin landlords know the dates their martins arrive each spring and leave each fall (or late summer), and many of them keep records of other key life cycle dates, noting the influx of each new group, the start of first nest-building, egg-laying, hatching and fledging.

And the interest of humans seems to be reciprocated.

Even in their wintering habits, purple martins seem influenced by human activities. Unlike most small migratory birds, most martins don't winter in the tropics (some do). Instead, they fly right on past the jungles of the Amazon and winter in a slightly more temperate area of farmlands, cities — and people. They winter chiefly in an area of southern Brazil not much larger than the state of Missouri.

And from this relatively small area they return each spring, some of them flying as much as 7,000 miles, to spread out over most of North America east of the Rockies, nesting in 37 states and parts of six Canadian provinces. (We're not sure yet where the martins of the far western states winter.)

Probably no aspect of the martin's life history is more interesting than its timetable — the linking of each phase of its life with an inner clock that drives it as much as 14,000 miles a year to associate so closely with humans in both halves of the hemisphere.

I've split this chapter into two major sections. The first deals with migration itself. The second deals with nesting activities, all of which occur during a four-month period of spring and summer in North America.

Subchapter A

Spring Migration

Columnist Leon Hale of the Houston Post once wrote:

"Spring begins, for me, the first day I hear purple martins sing.

"It began this year (1979) at Port O'Connor, at 3:30 p.m. Lately I've been roaming along the coast, and at Port O'Connor I had stopped to check my map and the singing came to me. All distant and gentle and so beautiful.

"The purple martin won't pound your ear, the way a blue jay does, or a mockingbird.

"The martin's song doesn't have much direction, either. When it reaches you, sometimes you have a hard time telling where it's coming from. It's like those birds spread it through the air, and it hangs up there in light clouds, and the notes travel in waves and surges, and fade, and return then from another direction.

"Port O'Connor has almost as many martin houses as human ones, and when the birds return their gentle singing fills the sky about that little city. Really nice to hear and I am pleased spring began for me there this year."

Hale is not alone. Spring begins for tens of thousands of persons the day they hear the first purple martin sing. That has been as early as January 1 in the Miami area and January 4 in south Texas. Those are the early dates from our records, although we have some late December sightings from south Florida, and it's quite possible some martins occasionally over-winter in that southern tip of our continent.

The first scouts traditionally are reported all along the Gulf coast during the month of January, with the very earliest reports from south Florida, south Texas and south Louisiana in that order. In very early February reports spread across the deep south and by mid-February are creeping into north Texas and the upper south states of Tennessee and North Carolina.

Throughout March reports come from the lower midwest and middle Atlantic, and throughout April from the upper midwest and lower New England. The final flurry of reports come in late April and early May from locations all across Canada, including the extreme northern limit of the range around Edmonton in central Alberta.

Scout reports — the very earliest arrivals — are useful, but they don't tell the whole story. In most parts of the range, birds don't begin staying at the sites for another week or so, and nesters continue to arrive for at least two months, with ASY birds generally arriving during the first of those months, and SY birds arriving during the second month.

Thousands of birds continue to migrate through southern areas where nesting is well underway.

In **Louisiana Birds**, George Lowery wrote, "We observe, for instance, the passage of purple martins even in the last half of April, when the birds of our own local colonies have been here for two months or more and are already beginning to incubate eggs. These late arrivals are possibly individuals bound for the extreme northern limits of the range, where spring is only then appearing."

Geographically, Purple Martin Junction is approximately in the center of the range, so let's use it as a typical case. These are the earliest sightings reported in Griggsville during the past 24 years:

1963: March 17	1975: March 21
1964: March 11	1976: March 24
1965: March 17	1977: March 19
1966: March 14	1978: March 18
1967: March 19	1979: March 29
1968: March 24	1980: March 13
1969: March 22	1981: March 12
1970: March 23	1982: March 20
1971: March 15	1983: April 4
1972: March 22	1984: March 28
1973: March 13	1985: March 27
1974: March 18	1986: March 14

Although scouts are usually seen for a brief period during the second half of March, the first "permanent" arrivals always show up during the first few days of April. These arrivals are more predictable than scouts. Scout sightings have ranged over a three-week variation, but most permanent arrivals have ranged over only a one-week variation.

At first only a dozen or so move in, always older birds and always a mixture of males and females, with males predominating.

Sometime in mid-April another small group will arrive, then another, and by May 1, a majority of ASY birds will be present. Some minor collecting of nest material may occur in April.

During the first two weeks of May, a major influx will occur, and most of them will be SY birds. SY birds will continue to filter in throughout May and into early June.

The period in which potential nesters arrive typically spans two months — in Griggsville that is early April to early June — and that span is somewhat longer in the south where warm weather starts earlier, and somewhat shorter in the north, where the season is shorter and nesters tend to get busy a little quicker.

Purple martins nest in these states and provinces east of the Rockies, but the range juts far to the northwest out of the upper left corner of this map, surrounding Edmonton in central Alberta. These are typical early spring arrival dates. In most areas, martins do not show up to stay for another 7-10 days.

Rather than publish a list of typical arrival dates for each state, we have included a map of typical dates. This seems a bit more useful. Just listing a date for each state can be misleading because of the north-south extension of some states. For example, scouts often show up at Russell Morgan's colony at Chester in southern Illinois as much as a month ahead of those at Nick Butler's home in the Chicago suburb of Lemont. And we've seen a range of two months between arrivals in south Texas and the Panhandle!

What influences them is a whole 'nother subject.

WHAT DETERMINES MOVEMENT?

Prevailing winds and temperatures are predominant factors in migration.

We don't have a typical picture of an entire migration period. We don't know how long a typical martin spends getting from Sao Paulo state to Illinois, for example. We don't know how continuous or broken that trip is, or even how direct a path they follow during the times they are flying.

But we do know their northward flights are stimulated by warm temperatures and favorable air currents. Many species move with favorable air fronts, and martins are no exceptions. At Purple Martin Junction, each new influx of martins almost always occurs after a day or two of warm air movement from the south or southwest. This has become so obvious over the years that new influxes are fairly predictable on certain days during April and May.

Swallows in general are daytime migrators, and we think martins follow this pattern, although martins have been reported moving at night. An interesting case of night movement reported from Fort Worth is discussed later in this chapter.

A majority of new arrivals are first noted at the Junction in the early morning, but because the site is usually not attended during the evening hours, we cannot say for certain some of these flights did not arrive the previous evening. We do know that some arrivals have occurred in the morning. So these either flew at night or stopped somewhere nearby late the previous day and came on in at sunrise.

When we understand all the factors influencing migration, maybe we will know what causes abnormal cases, such as individuals moving northward far too early to have a chance of surviving. This occasionally occurs. Take the case of one overeager Minnesota bird, for example:

On March 3, 1973, Rev. Arne Carlson of Fisher, Minnesota, reported a scout at William Wagner's colony. Normal arrival at this location near Grand Forks in northwestern Minnesota is April 14-17. But there was no mistaking this report, for on April 5, still a trifle early for scouts in that area, a martin was found dead in that house, and had been dead for some time, even though the house had been cleaned the previous fall.

(During that same season, martins appeared in Griggsville on March 13, one of the earliest dates on record, and Hellen Ochs of Columbus, Indiana, reported scouts there February 24, also very unusual.)

We don't know how long the trip takes, but it can't take longer than two months. They typically spend five months in their nesting areas (including assembly time), and three months at their wintering sites, so this allows no more than four months of each year for the two long flights.

In 1985, a martin marked in Barretos, Sao Paulo state, was recovered near Dallas less than seven weeks later. We don't know when it left

This is the view from the studio of television station KTXS in Abilene, Texas, and this is the house that was involved in a weird series of events. In 1976, at the precise moment the new house was introduced to viewers by Michael Henry Martin on his show, Henry's Den, the first martin sailed into the picture and landed on the house — the kind of coincidence TV personalities can talk about for weeks. Later in the season, however, the house — which two pairs had moved into — was stolen. It was replaced later that year, and on the following April 16, 1977, the first bird of a new colony showed up at the house on the same day that Martin's first baby was born. The little girl was named April Martin.

Barretos or when it arrived in Dallas, but now at least know that this 4,000-mile trip can be made in less than seven weeks.

Jean Dorst, in **The Migration of Birds**, made these general remarks about migrants: "Migrants traveling overland seem to tarry along the way and to progress in stages, with rest stops in between which may last a day or more. An average 'day's' flight (often by night) is from 90 to 155 miles, which represents only six to eight hours in the air. Some migrants average only 65 miles a day." This leisurely and broken pattern seems consistent with what we know about martins, but they have the ability to fly hundreds of miles a day if necessary.

In Doppler radar tests in 1963 and 1964 at the University of Michigan Biological Station, Gary Schnell gauged martin speeds on windless days in a range up to 41 miles per hour. He recorded speeds of 169 martins flying near their colony and noted a range of speeds from 5-41 miles per hour, with a mean of 21.7. Dorst lists the average speed of purple martins at 20 mph.

Further, the average speed noted by Schnell among all those Michigan birds we mentioned earlier trying to find their way back home was only a little over 7 mph, and the top speed was only a little over 27.

But Dorst also noted that migrating birds and birds flying in flocks travel faster than normal. He attributed this to "psychological" reasons. Obviously, birds in flocks are more certain about where they are going.

THE MYSTERY OF MIGRATION

One of the great unexplained mysteries of the world is the exact method or methods by which birds find their way on great migration odysseys and manage to return to their exact starting points. Do martins use landmarks, the sun and stars, the earth's magnetic field, an instinctive sense of direction, or a combination of all of these? Probably the martins don't understand it themselves.

"Why" is as much a question as "how." The major theories as to why birds migrate include the northern and southern ancestral home theories, and the continental drift theory. In brief, these are as follows:

The northern ancestral home theory contends that all of the northern areas were tropical at some period in history, and that birds flourished uniformly throughout the area. As the great ice cap descended over the continent, it drove the birds ahead of it. As the ice cap receded, the birds attempted to follow it northward into their ancestral homes, but with each winter they were driven south again.

The theory of southern ancestry holds that all birds originated in the tropical central areas, and that overflow from these areas caused the northern areas to be populated, but that many of these birds must still return to the tropical areas during the colder parts of the year.

The theory of continental drift holds that the northern and southern land masses originally were one but drifted into segments. The separation gradually developed the long migration routes as extensions of age-old flight patterns that originally were much shorter.

None of these theories is universally endorsed.

Nor is any theory about why they start to move when they do. Why, for example do they begin both the spring and fall migrations during periods when food abounds where they already are? What tells them it is time to go?

The theory of photoperiodism holds that migration is induced by the length of the day and the quantity of light to which the bird is exposed each day, and that birds move south in response to the shortening of the day.

Could it be that weather conditions in other regions influence the decision to begin migration? At the time of the autumnal equinox, weather in the Caribbean and Gulf of Mexico is often in a state of turmoil. Hurricanes are not uncommon and other tropical storms keep air masses in wildly erratic motion. Perhaps the birds have some sense that warns them of future turbulent conditions.

Perhaps they are aware of relationships between the upper and lower atmospheres. Do the speed and path of the jet stream herald either autumns of calm weather in the Gulf, or warn of violent winds and rains?

We have seen proof that birds are more aware of subtle environmental conditions than humans. One day in the late '60s, several of us were in uptown Griggsville around noon when we noticed the martins behaving in an unusual manner. They were all flying rather high above the city and with an intensity that had an unusual attitude about it. We asked each other "What's wrong with those martins?" and were particularly puzzled because it was a beautiful day.

Three hours later one of the most violent and destructive storms in decades hit the city.

Just as science has not settled on the "why," there is disagreement on the "how." How do birds find their way along routes covering thousands of miles over the curvature of the earth, sometimes over land, sometimes over water?

It is commonly believed that ground-feeding birds whose migratory flights take place at night find their unerring way by using a form of celestial navigation.

Dr. William Beecher of Chicago made an extensive study of migratory habits and subscribed to both the theories of celestial navigation and photoperiodism. In a discussion of general aspects of migration, he said:

"When the endocrine system of a migratory bird has been activated by the increasing hours of daylight in the spring, he must go! If you confine him in a cage, then all night, while his wild brothers are migrating overhead, he will face the proper direction, as if in a trance, and flutter his wings!

"My friend, Franz Sauer, the German ornithologist, devised a cage in which captive European warblers could see only the star-filled night sky and showed that they are able to navigate by the stars. This was double-checked by bringing them inside a planetarium in which the orientation of the starlit sky could be changed at will. Radar seems to show that migrants become bewildered in overcasts, but we do not know whether this confusion is due to the absence of stars or the presence of city lights, man's greatest contribution to migration hazards."

Light from certain stars — and perhaps the moon — impinging on the sight sensors as certain angles could guide these birds on an accurate course to their destinations. Light from the sun may be used similarly by daytime-flying birds like martins.

Dr. Beecher said that migratory patterns, as well as all other knowledge a bird will need for survival, are present in the egg, and that the migratory pattern a bird inherits ". . .is a flight direction; birds carried hundreds of miles to the right or left of the normal route still fly in the same direction, but they do not arrive at the intended goal. . ."

While we don't know exactly what triggers the process, we know its first signs. Prior to migration, birds undergo at least two internal changes. The size of the sex organs begins to increase and the amount of body fat starts to expand — the fat to be used later as an energy reserve.

Birds that make long non-stop flights tend to store more fat than do the more leisurely migrators. Martins, according to Kathy Klimkiewicz, are among those species that do not store a large amount of fat. This tends to support the belief of those who say martins don't normally fly across the Gulf of Mexico. That's a question we will talk about more at the tail end of this chapter in a discussion of routes.

Fall Migration

The season begins to wane in June along the Gulf Coast, in July in the midwest and mid-Atlantic, in August in the north.

As the young fledge and families spend progressively more time away from houses, small flocks develop and soon become large flocks. As the final attachment to their houses falls away, they mass into pre-migration flocks numbering in thousands and roost in trees and on wires, usually along waterways where food is plentiful.

Fall migration is then at hand. We'll discuss those flocks shortly, but first a few remarks on the process of assembling.

Traditionally, purple martins both young and old are thought to fly northward before beginning their southern flight. We don't know whether that is standard practice, but many do.

In late July and early August of the years 1975, 1976 and 1977, Charles Brown of Sherman, Texas, and Sam D. Wolfe III of Nacogdoches, Texas, visited a martin assembly flock at Tishomongo National Wildlife Refuge in Oklahoma. Each year they found evidence of the presence of birds they had banded during those respective seasons near Sherman 50 miles south of Tishomongo. In addition, they had made visual observations of many martins flying north over Lake Texoma's Preston Peninsula, headed in the direction of Tishomongo.

We occasionally have News readers report seeing martins flying north after complete nesting, and ask why they are flying north. "Are they going to raise another brood where it is cooler?"

It is safe to say they are not going to raise another brood. It's almost as safe to say they are flying north to join assembly flocks. Why north, we don't know, unless it's their way of programming their young on the direction they will have to fly next spring to get here from South America.

Or maybe it's as simple as this: If birds in every flock assemble from all directions, then **some** of them have to come from the south.

We usually do not know where birds from Purple Martin Junction congregate. A few years we have observed assembly flocks in the vicinity of LaGrange lock and dam on the Illinois River 20 miles northeast of Griggsville, and another year near Naples, also on the Illinois, about eight miles northeast of Griggsville. We presume our birds were parts of those flocks.

Northern flocks often remain at peak numbers for two weeks or so, then begin to decline and are completely gone within another week. Southern

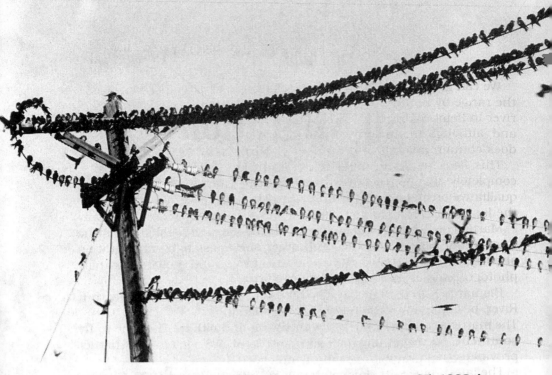

This assembly group was photographed August 25, 1983, in Bismarck, North Dakota, by Ed Bry of the North Dakota Game and Fish Department. Martins are typically gone from that Missouri River community by September 1.

flocks usually remain longer than northern flocks and are larger on the average.

The 1985 reports from Brewton, Alabama, and Keokuk, Iowa, sharply illustrate the differences one is apt to find between assembly flocks in the south and north.

Weldon Vickery of Atmore, Alabama, keeps track of the annual activity near Brewton, at a paper mill complex belonging to Container Corporation of America. Vickery estimated that flock at 25,000-50,000 on June 20, with the actual total probably much closer to the upper figure.

He said first birds fledge in his area near the Gulf around May 15, and that is the time first birds begin to gather at the roost site. He estimated 1,000 birds there on May 15, 1985. He said the number builds gradually and peaks around July 4 or shortly after. Then numbers begin to decrease as groups leave each day.

While 50,000 isn't unusual in the south, a flock of 5,000 can be a pretty big deal in our area of Illinois.

Bob Cecil of Keokuk, 60 miles northwest of Griggsville, reported a flock there on the Mississippi that was "the largest I've heard about in the midwest" (in 1985). He keeps careful records on this flock every year, said it numbered 6,000 in 1984, but that it was "way over that so far and still growing" on August 8.

We can get a clue to behavior of flocks at the extreme northern fringe of the range by noting the swallow flock that gathers each year along the river in Pembroke, Ontario. This flock totals as many as 115,000 birds and, although the majority are usually tree, barn and bank swallows, it does contain a significant number of purple martins.

This flock peaks in mid-August and then declines until the site is completely abandoned in early September. Observers there don't have a qualitative breakdown on the departures, but I suspect martins are among the last to leave.

Martins do not start assembling in Bismarck, North Dakota, until mid-August, but peak during the fourth week and are gone by September 1 or shortly after. At least that was the case with a group of 2,000 photographed in 1983 by Ed Bry of North Dakota Game and Fish.

Bismarck is in the heart of North Dakota on the banks of the Missouri River, but it is at approximately the same latitude as Pembroke, Ontario. The martin's range juts far to the northwest in the Great Plains part of the continent, so many thousands of martins from the Canadian prairie provinces pass through North Dakota each year.

The latest departure dates in our records from the northern ranges are from the northeast. In 1972, Napoleon Beaudet reported a single martin from the big colony of Arthur Belleau at St. Redempteur near Quebec City did not leave until October 9. By then, night temperatures were dipping to freezing, although daytime temperatures were considerably warmer.

Beaudet noted that martins normally left that northern St. Lawrence region in mid-August, but that in 1969, the flocks has remained until late September. In 1968 he had watched martins leave at the end of September from Villa Manrese in the very heart of Quebec City.

The latest northern case in our records is from that year of 1969. On October 23, a pair of martins was still in one of the houses in the Phil Downeys' colony in Point du Chene in eastern New Brunswick. They were trying to get a late-hatching young martin to fly.

The birds had a little help during a cold snap that year, when the Downeys had laid dead insects on the house porches and — much to their surprise — the martins had accepted them and stayed alive. Eight other young martins had flown successfully from that house on September 22, about the time the late arrival was hatching.

The Downeys never learned the fate of that devoted pair of parents, however. The young bird died the following day and the parents disappeared. They presumably migrated, but the Downeys had no way of knowing how successfully.

Late October, when those birds left New Brunswick, is usually the late date for flocks to leave Florida, and the first date for arrivals in the wintering grounds of Sao Paulo — 7,000 miles from New Brunswick.

Even though southern martins nest earlier and start to assemble earlier, many remain in that area throughout the summer.

Flocks have been reported in Florida as late as November, but in these extreme cases we suspect these are northern birds moving through and that the flocks from that area have long since departed.

Season-long assembly flocks are unheard of in the north. Occasionally we hear of such a flock in the south, and it may be common, but we have had no occasion to check any of these reports.

The most imposing report was made by Leon Hale several years ago in his column. He told of up to 100,000 martins roosting each year at the Rohm and Haas chemical plant near Houston — about a half-mile from the Houston ship channel.

Hale said these martins roost there throughout the season, and reach a peak in July.

He obtained most of his information from A. D. Sharpton, who had worked in the area 25 years and at the time was working as a gate guard. He liked martins but, like other personnel at the plant was not enthusiastic about the droppings on the ground. They wished some of the martins would roost elsewhere.

Sharpton said most of the roosting birds during the nesting season were males, and that females spent their nights in the nests until young were ready to fly. (Normally, males and females both spend their nights in the houses if there is room, otherwise males roost nearby.)

Another large flock that gathered each year at the Mobil refinery at Beaumont, did not begin to gather until July, according to Joe Combs of the Beaumont Enterprise. These martins gathered on warm pipes, and in 1974, Combs reflected on this: ". . .literally thousands gather there late every afternoon. They sleep on the warm pipes and supports, so close together they are almost 'elbow to elbow.' Their night roosting place would be impossible for a human being, due to the excessive heat. But the purple martins love the heat for some reason. They come back every summer to the same place they have come every summer for several years." Different theories have been advanced for their choice of warm steam-filled air. It has been suggested they shed their mites. . .that can't stand the heat and fall off. In that way they free themselves of vermin and have a pleasant trip back to the jungles, as they cross the Gulf of Mexico. There is no proof of this, but it makes good gossip.

I find it curious that heat, which can be so hard on young birds in the nest, can be so welcome at times to the older birds.

In 1973, T. A. Dillard of Charleston, Tennessee, photographed an assembly he estimated at 100,000 birds. These, like many such groups, were on utility wires near the Hiwassee River in the cities of Charleston and Calhoun.

Dillard wrote: "This has been an assembly area for many years, but the number of purple martins using the area this year was much larger than in the past. It is estimated that at one time there was in excess of 100,000 martins in this area.

"This area is located in part of a residential development along the river. The only problem encountered with this large number of birds is their droppings which cover streets and the lawns under utility lines. The residents seem to tolerate this because they realize the helpfulness of the martins as insect catchers."

Citizens are not always that tolerant.

One early account reported in National Museum Bulletin 179 states:

"Another trait of the martin that has long attracted attention and produced much writing is its communal roosting habit late in summer, when the species gathers in great flocks preparatory to and during migration. Concentrations up to 100,000 birds have been noted, and the attendant noise sometimes results in such a nuisance to people that direct efforts are made against the birds and many killed in various methods. To some degree these roosts are a parallel to those of the vanished passenger

This picture, which appeared in my first book, was taken in 1962 by the Chicago Tribune and shows an assembly flock near Lake Michigan on the city's north side. Although martins are not usually associated with large cities in many enthusiasts' minds, large numbers do exist in large metropolitan areas. While most of them seem to be in the suburbs, a few nest in more central areas, too. I don't know whether martins really favor the more outlying areas or housing opportunities simply don't exist in the central areas.

pigeon in that branches of trees are broken by the weight of the birds and, as Arthur T. Wayne (1910) puts it, the noise produced by such a multitude resembled the sound of escaping steam. In 1905 a huge roost at Wrightsville Beach (near Wilmington), N.C. was attacked by irate citizens and 8,000 to 15,000 birds were killed. The North Carolina Audubon Society succeeded in convicting 12 of the offenders, who were fined."

I mentioned this incident in my first book and it caught the attention of Eddie Earwood of Wrightsville Beach, who thought that mark in his community's history ought to be cancelled. So in 1985, with the assistance of Mayor Fran Russ, Wrightsville Beach held "Welcome Back, Purple Martins" Day on March 21. I join many others in tipping my hat to Wrightsville Beach.

Other accounts were mentioned in Bulletin 179:

"G. Clyde Fisher (1907) describes a roost near Quincy, Fla., which he estimated to contain 5,000 birds and, like Wayne, was impressed with the noise, which he also described as being 'much like escaping steam.'

"A typical roost, and a very well known one, was that at Cape May, N.J., written of in detail by Witmer Sone (1937). Students should peruse his account with great interest. It is too long to quote here, and since 1936 the roost has been deserted not only by martins but by robins, starlings and grackles. However, it may sometime again be instituted, and extracts of Stone's account are given herewith:

"'For many years it (the roost) was located on the Physick property on the principal street of the town. Here there is a grove of silver maples about thirty feet in height and covering an area of some two acres, growing so close together that their tops join one another, making a dense canopy with constant shade. . .Were it not for this roost, the only one in South Jersey so far as I know, martin history at Cape May would come to a close early in August when the last of the fledglings become self dependent and sail away with their parents. But as it is, though there may be days in August when practically no martins are to be found for miles around Cape May from sunrise to sunset, they will gather in ever in-creasing numbers to pass the night in this small grove which, so far as our eyes can detect, offers no advantages over hundreds of similar groves past which the birds must have flown.'"

Although martins are presumed to be daytime migrants, at least some departures occur during the dark of night. Weldon Vickery has seen many small groups from that Atmore, Alabama, site departing around 3-3:30 a.m.

And Mrs. Richard Vannoy of Fort Worth watched a flock depart at sundown, presumably to begin migration. In 1976 she wrote, "We were quite lucky this year. We discovered their departure tree. For weeks, they gathered in a large, 50-ft.-high cottonwood tree. We alerted all our martin friends and our TV station, KXAS. On the night of the departure, there were between five and seven thousand birds.

"We had been watching them for days as the flock grew larger. Then, on this particular night, instead of going into the tree, they kept circling, picking up late strays. Quite suddenly, the group took off for the southeast. This was August 19."

WHERE DO THEY WINTER?

The centuries-old question of exactly where martins spend their winters was at least partially answered in 1984, and the answer was simple and surprising.

Long presumed to winter mainly in the Amazon basin, huge numbers of martins — perhaps most of them — winter instead in the well populated southern Brazilian state of Sao Paulo. Many flocks roost at night in the center of cities, and are so conspicuous some cities have considered them nuisances.

For years they had been misidentified as gray-breasted martins. This is a common, essentially non-migratory species common from northern Argentina through Central America and part of Mexico. It appears almost identical to Progne subis, except that both sexes look like female purple martins.

Sao Paulo is among Brazil's leading states in both manufacturing and agriculture. Much of that industry is in the city of Sao Paulo, which is home to around 12 million persons and according to the United Nations, could have 26 million citizens by the year 2000 and rank second among the world's cities.

Much of the state is agricultural, however. Miles and miles of gently rolling interior countryside are covered with plantations of sugarcane, coffee, corn and orchards. With the exception of plantation and related housing, few homes sit isolated in the countryside as in North America, but many cities dot the interior. Most cities have a central business and religious district built around a beautifully landscaped plaza, and some of these are well lighted. Mercury lights are becoming common.

Purple martins seem drawn to these plazas at night, presumably because they are well lighted. Such a flock in 1984 in the city of Rio Preto (Sao Jose do Rio Preto) stirred a controversy that may have initiated a new era for the martin in Brazil.

Rio Preto is a city of 135,000, a beautiful city built by the coffee industry some 240 miles northwest of Sao Paulo. It was plagued by a flock of some 70,000 martins. Firecrackers didn't work. Shopkeepers, taxi drivers and street vendors were calling for stronger measures.

The debate attracted the attention of Dalgas Frisch, vice president of the Brazilian Association of Preservation of Wildlife. He learned the flocks were purple martins — Progne subis — that they migrated to North America where citizens erected houses for them, and that while in Brazil they performed a valuable service — very valuable indeed.

This is where many of them go. . .

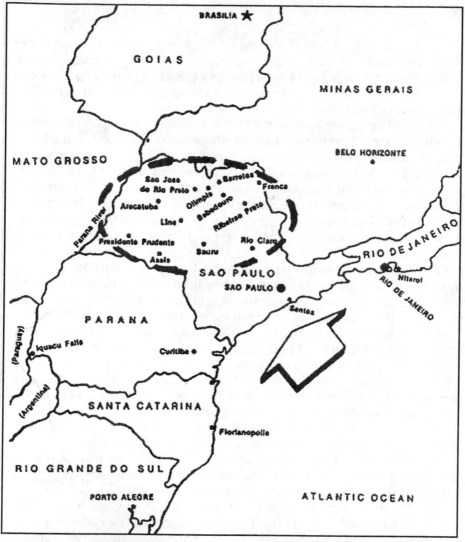

A substantial part of North America's purple martin population winters in the southern Brazilian state of Sao Paulo. This state covers more than 95,000 square miles, but the part of the state in which they are most heavily concentrated is smaller — about the size of Missouri or Oklahoma. In 1984, flocks were studied in 12 cities listed on this map, and Dalgas Frisch said these represented only a small part of the total wintering population. While this state contains the world's fourth largest city (Sao Paulo, 12 million), much of it is gently rolling countryside covered with sugarcane, corn and coffee plantations and orchards, and dotted with smaller cities. In some ways it resembles the North American areas in which a majority of martins nest.

Frisch learned the martins foraged every day over cane and coffee plantations and consumed enormous numbers of insects, including two very important crop pests — a soybean moth and cane parasite — as well as mosquitoes. Moreover, their presence in Brazil occurred just at the time these insects most commonly lay eggs.

Realizing that martins are too valuable to citizens of both continents to be exterminated, Frisch launched an educational campaign that made a quick and effective start on changing public attitudes toward martins.

Starting in December, when the flocks were just starting to reach their peaks, his campaign included newspaper articles, posters and videotape features shown nationwide on the Globo television network. While citizens interviewed **before** the campaign were universal in condemning the birds, those interviewed **after** the campaign were almost as unanimous in praising them.

Along with the educational campaign, Frisch's organization started working to lessen the problems caused by flocks. They discovered that by regulating the time at which various city lights were turned on they could move at least one flock from one roost location to another. By delaying the turn-on of lights in critical areas by as little as a half-hour, the birds could be attracted to well lighted trees in less sensitive areas — at least in the limited testing they were able to do.

At the same time, they persuaded some persons to move taxi stands and popcorn machines short distances to more favorable locations, and in one case persuaded a city to make changes in traffic routing.

The result, says Frisch, is that the nuisance was made very minimal, while the great good the birds do was allowed to continue.

Frisch believes purple martins winter in Sao Paulo because it is most like North American regions in which many nest. This means agricultural land with many small to medium sized cities.

The climate is warmer than most North American nesting regions, however. Being just north of the Tropic of Capricorn, its climate is more like that of Cuba, southern Florida, or other areas near the Tropic of Cancer. January-February temperatures are typically 100 degrees or more, and in July — the depth of winter — temperatures drop only into the 50s and 60s.

Frisch theorized the population is growing because of the expansion of housing in North America. He said the Rio Preto flock numbered only 2,500 a few years ago, but had reached 50,000 when his project was launched in 1983-84 (and reached 70,000 in 1984-85). Censusing of the Sao Paulo flocks has not been done enough years, however, to determine whether this is real growth or a shift in distribution of wintering populations.

Although the southern Brazil population may represent most martins, it is obviously not the only wintering population. Some birds do winter in the Amazon and almost certainly in a number of areas scattered across

Abra seu coração a quem voou 10 mil quilômetros para ver você!

Ela é o equilíbrio entre a agricultura e a natureza. Proteja-a.

Comind   **TRANS BRASIL**   **TAM**   repro

Dalgas Frisch used big (16"x23"), bright yellow posters to gain acceptance for the flocks that were beginning to wear out their welcome in the cities of southern Brazil. Translated from Portuguese, it means, "Open your heart to who flew 10,000 kilometers to visit you."

extreme northern South America. We'll go into this a bit later in this chapter when routes are discussed.

HISTORY OF A MISCONCEPTION

Purple martins have been treasured in North America since pre-colonial times. Indians put up gourds. Early white settlers put up simple wooden houses, and later farmers built more elaborate wooden houses. Modern enthusiasts use a wide array of housing. Tens of thousands of human homes have houses for these semi-domesticated swallows.

Information on their wintering areas has been scarce, however. During the past century, a few legbands have been recovered, and these recovery locations have been scattered all over the northern two-thirds of South America east of the Andes, from Uruguay in the south to the Guyanas in the north. The Amazon River itself seemed to be the focus.

Alexander Sprunt's respected 1942 study, for example, said, "During the winter season these birds are apparently concentrated chiefly in the Amazon Valley of Brazil (Manaqueri, Barra do Rio Negro, and Itaituba). They have been found also at this season in the coastal regions of Brazil (San Luiz, Rosario, Rio de Janeiro, and Iguape). One banded (B-219327) at Winona, Minn. in May 1934 was recovered in December 1936 near Para, Brazil." (Para is now known as Belem and is a large city on the northeast coast near the Para River mouth.)

The Allen-Nice study in 1952 did not deal in any detail with the wintering range, and the Johnston-Hardy study of 1962 ("Behavior of the Purple Martin") did not get into that subject at all.

Most recent studies by researchers have accepted the Amazon assumption, perhaps because original research in South America is too expensive for most people to consider. In a 1981 article in Natural History magazine, Charles R. Brown of Princeton wrote, "Purple martins migrate through Central America and the Caribbean to the Amazon River basin of Brazil, where they winter."

In 1974, in response to an inquiry from the Nature Society, Helio Ferraz de Almeida Camargo of the Zoological Museum of the University of Sao Paulo wrote:

"In his catalog (Aves do Brasil, 1944, vol. 2) Oliverio Pinto mentions that P. subis occurs in several localities in the northern and eastern regions of Brazil, coming from USA and Canada.

"To these localities, I would add, according to the existing material in our collection:

"1 male, collected at Fordlandia (right bank of Rio Tapajos) State of Para, in February 7, 1965.

"2 males, collected at Urucurituba (left bank of Rio Tapajos) State of Para, in January 7, 1965.

"3 males, collected at Lake Tarumazinho (vicinity of Manaus) State of Amazonas, in November 17-18, 1967.

"Judging from the occurrences given above, it seems that P. subis lives in humid areas in Brazil."

(The state of Para is a huge part of the Amazon basin fronting on the Atlantic Ocean; the state of Amazonas is also a chunk of the Amazon basin, but farther inland.)

In our own Nature Society records, we can find only one record of a South American recovery being reported by any of the banders who read the News. In April, 1983, Rebecca Dellinger of Duncanville, Texas, reported that one of the martins banded by Tom Dellinger in 1979 had been recovered at Manaus, on the river in the very heart of the Amazon basin.

HOW DO THEY GET THERE?

There are three general routes by which birds can enter North America from the south, and many persons have felt that martins use all three. They are the Mexican land route: Yucatan-to-Gulf coast water route; and eastern Caribbean island-hopping route.

I have long believed they use all three routes, based on the spotty evidence that has been available, but some observers in recent years have been leaning toward the belief that virtually all of them use the Mexican route.

They base this on such evidence as the usually casual migration habits of the martin, hard evidence that at least some eastern birds do fly to the southwest and use the Mexican route, plus more or less plausible ways to explain the evidence for the other two routes.

So let's look at the evidence for and against all three routes.

ISLAND-HOPPING

Use of a route through Florida and the Caribbean islands seems obvious to me because our first reports each year normally are from southern Florida. That area beats southern Texas by a few days and southern Louisiana by yet a few more days.

While some martins have been discovered wintering in Florida, these must be exceptions. If a substantial population wintered there, they would be obvious, even in the Everglades.

We've had reports from persons who watched martins moving south in Florida in late summer and fall. But one of the more reliable and interesting reports was from Tom Morrill, who lives five miles south of Tallahassee on the northern edge of the Appalachicola National Forest. In 1982 he wrote, "Today, July 7, I'm a take-it-easy southerner sitting on the porch of our cabin 20 miles east of the place on the cypress pond. I'm looking south down a broad river under about a fourth of the sky. All day, any time I've looked with binoculars, martins have been visible flying south. Mostly they seem to be singles though each part of a giant migrating pattern.

"It's wonderful to realize these are children of good martin people up the country. . ." he concluded.

What is interesting about this report is that all three options are available to these martins. They are approaching the Gulf at the bend of Florida, and a glance at the map shows they could turn right toward Mexico, left toward Florida, or go straight ahead toward Yucatan some 600 miles away.

Strangely, no one can yet say with 100 percent certainty which way they do go. There does appear to be movement over water, but debate goes on whether it is by design or accident.

Red Marston reported the following story in 1982 in the St. Petersburg Times: "In May, 1981, (Hal Cavenaugh) was delivering a sailboat from Mobile to Clearwater. He had just checked his position as being 100 miles out from the Pensacola 'farewell' buoy. Then his attention was attracted by a bird, a purple martin that flew close by the boat, circled then landed on the deck. Shortly afterwards, a second purple martin came and landed. Eventually, there were 38 martins aboard, wobbly legged and obviously exhausted. Some made their way into the cabin area.

"Cavenaugh tried to feed the birds with bits of bread. But the offering did not appeal to them. . .As the days passed, the martins began to die. By the time the sailboat was coming into the pass at Clearwater Beach, only four were left. Then one flew away. Soon afterward the remaining three headed for nearby land.

"Purple martins winter in South America, thus do considerable open-water flying. Perhaps they were returning to the upper Gulf of Mexico when a storm delayed them with strong head winds. . ."

Perhaps.

The Brewton, Alabama, flock is in an ideal location to tell us something about migration routes. Like Tom Morrill's migrant martins a bit farther east, these birds have all three options open to them. If any birds fly directly across the Gulf, these surely do.

Weldon Vickery had not been successful in tracing the route of departing birds, as of the 1985 season, although he had seen numerous groups depart. Small flocks often leave at 3-3:30 a.m., he said.

At that hour of the morning, they're a bit hard to keep track of. He is handicapped by being about 40 miles from the coast. Even if these birds fly directly south to the coast, that does not necessarily mean they will not turn, upon reaching the coast, and follow it one way or the other.

He believes they fly directly across the Gulf or down the Florida coast, but is sure he will eventually determine conclusively which route they use.

Vickery said he has had no reports from persons observing fall migration, but men working on oil rigs 30-40 miles out in the Gulf often report martins on their rigs in spring, usually in late February or March. The rigs "really get wrapped up with 'em," according to oil workers.

I am still certain that substantial numbers of martins do migrate through Florida, but am willing to concede that they may all be from the southeastern states and that those from the middle Atlantic and New England regions move southwest through Mexico.

I know that some Florida migration is a fact, and it is apt to occur over an extended period. Several years ago, for example, Ken Bower Sr. filed the following report from Sebring:

"We are still seeing groups of martins feeding and flying south. Today (December 26) my family and I saw another group. We live in the south-central part of Florida in the country on Lake Josephine, and there are as many bugs to eat now as in the summer. But by the time they get to Brazil it will be time to turn around."

Well, maybe not. The birds that migrate through Florida may winter in northern South America, which probably is no more than 2-3 weeks away. Or maybe they winter in Cuba or other islands.

Or maybe Florida itself, where some observers, including Allan Harrison, have reported martins apparently overwintering.

Harrison, a biologist and News columnist who's very knowledgeable about birds, lives in Tampa and twice has definitely identified martins in the Tampa area during every month of the year. The most recent of these included the winter of 1974-75, after which he commented, "Without being too certain or dogmatic about it, this might suggest that a few birds do indeed winter here."

And aberrant individuals may overwinter in other southern locations, too. In 1956, according to George Lowrey, Father J. L. Dorn studied 11 martins in a flock of tree swallows near New Orleans on December 26 and 27.

Which brings us to the Yucatan question.

This question seemed to have been settled 30 years ago with accounts of martins seen over the Gulf at night, including some exhausted birds landing on a ship 60 miles south of the Louisiana coast. In 1952 Bullis and Lincoln described heavy concentrations of land birds, including martins, on the U.S. Fish and Wildlife's ship, the Oregon.

In 1926, pictures were taken of hundreds of martins that had been forced to land on the S.S. West Quechee 125 miles south of the Louisiana coast. And there have been other reports, as well as numerous observations of martins landing on the Louisiana-Mississippi coast exhausted after storms. (During favorable weather migrants do not land on the coast but go on inland, a phenomenon known as the coastal "hiatus.")

But critics of the Gulf theory have contended that these birds recorded during storms were over the Gulf precisely because of the storms. . .that they were blown off course from their normal land routes.

But how about the experience of Wade Bailey, captain of a fishing boat operating in the Gulf of Mexico? In the spring of 1986, he recorded martins landing on his ship every night from April 22 through May 16. His locations during those periods were about 150 miles south by southwest of New Orleans and about 170 miles southeast of New Orleans. He said he had no doubt about the identifications and the period could have been longer but he was in port for a week at either end of the above period. Although a few rainy days occurred during the period, storms could not have accounted for all of these birds.

Kathy Klimkiewicz is convinced they do not normally use the long-distance water route, mainly because martins do not build up fat stores prior to migration in the way typical of species that are known to migrate long distances over water. In the scientific study of natural history, this type of evidence carries a lot of weight because in nature hardly anything happens without a good reason — a good survival reason.

The island-hopping routes open to Florida martins do not involve any single segment as long as the Yucatan jump. In fact, birds can fly southwest from the southern tip of Florida to the western end of Cuba and on to Yucatan in two short leaps, neither one of which exceeds 100 miles.

Finally, the Mexican route is so well established that we don't even need to discuss it here. The only question that remains is what percentage of all martins migrate through Mexico.

BANDING HAS HELPED

Until recently, researchers have depended on legbands to learn about migration patterns, and although some valuable information has been obtained this way, many efforts have led only to frustrations.

Typical were the results of Baxter B. Wilson of Charlotte, North Carolina. During a five-year period — 1956-61 — Wilson and a registered bander, Dr. William Anderson, banded 474 martins at Wilson's colony at Steele Creek Nursery. Only 17 were ever seen and recovered, and the information they learned fell far short of their hopes.

In a letter to the Nature Society, Wilson reviewed the project:

"The banding project left most of my questions unanswered, but I think I was able to glean a little information. . .We alternated each year from the right to the left leg to give us some idea of which birds were returning. . .

"When I began the banding operation there were four questions I wanted answered: 1. How do martins from Piedmont, Carolina, go to the coast and on to South America? 2. Do the birds mate for life or remate each year? 3. What is the life span? 4. Do the young return to the same colony with the adults or return on their own in a haphazard manner?

"In my banding experience I learned nothing factual as to question number one. . .

"I had at least hoped to find which route our birds take to the coast. I have observed large congregating, or nesting, places at the mouth of the Cape Fear River near Wilmington, NC (Holden Beach), along the Santee-Cooper (Charleston, SC) and have seen what seemed to be hundreds of thousands around New Orleans. From this I would conclude that they follow the natural waterways flowing from the location of their colony to the coast. Using the Appalachian range as a dividing line, this would have the martins east of the range going down to the Florida east coast and crossing the Gulf from the west coast of Florida. All martins from west of the Appalachians would follow the natural Mississippi flow to the New Orleans area and then across the Gulf or by land to Central America. My greatest disappointment with the project was that I could prove NONE of the above. I had hoped that a band would possibly be found in the Charleston area, another around Jacksonville, Florida, another on the Gulf and then I would have a real theory.

"As for question number two, I get a big fat zero. I was never able to get two banded birds to mate with each other.

"I did find that the life span is up to at least seven years, as I had this one male to return to the same compartment for six straight years. This also definitely proves that the same birds do come back year after year.

"The banding threw some definite light on the question of the one-year birds returning independently of the adults and the banding experiment pretty well proves this point. Since I have been observing martins I have noticed that they come in three main waves. Here, the first drift in from around March 1-15; the next, the largest group, comes in from April 1-15. By this date, most of the adults will be in but very few of the young birds.

"In my detailed log of 15 years I noted only one time that I saw a one-year male as early as April 10. The one-year birds continue to come in from around April 15 to May 20.

"I noted that many one-year birds do not nest the first year. In a large colony there are always several one-year males who do not get a mate and often will build a flimsy nest by themselves.

"From this I would conclude that the one-year birds will follow the same migration paths of their parents but that the few who return to the same colony of their birth do so largely by chance. This is probably the reason that so many first-year martin houses are stocked with one-year birds.

"Out of the 474 birds banded I noted from my journal that only 17 banded birds were ever seen again."

Banding has been an enormously valuable tool in the study of birds, but on the question of where martins go and how they get there the application of tens of thousands of bands over a period of several decades had not produced the big answers.

In 1985 a new technique was introduced.

THE ULTRAVIOLET PROJECT

In the early 1980s, Ed Knittle and other researchers of the Denver Wildlife Research Center had experimented with the use of ultraviolet-sensitive paint in studying the migration habits of blackbirds in the Great Plains.

In this procedure, flocks are sprayed with an invisible mist that contains paint pigments visible only under ultraviolet light. Although birds are unaware of its presence, this pigment adheres to feathers for at least eight months and is usually detectable until the feathers are lost through molt.

In 1984 the Nature Society, U.S. Fish and Wildlife and Brazilian Association for Preservation of Wildlife decided to see what this new technique could tell us about martin migration.

In late January, 1985, the Brazilian group, led by Dalgas Frisch and using equipment and personnel supplied by Engesa, a military contractor, sprayed five large flocks in the Sao Paulo cities of Araraquara, Barretos, Ribeirao Preto, Rio Claro and Sao Jose do Rio Preto. A different color was used in each city.

Spraying was done at night and martins were "spooked" from the trees long enough to fly through the mist. A high percentage of birds were marked.

In total, approximately 250,000 martins were sprayed.

As soon as the spraying was completed, a U.S. team consisting of Knittle and Klimkiewicz from the U.S. Fish and Wildlife Service, and Tom Coulson and Jamie Hill from the Nature Society arrived to help check the quality of the marking and do some preliminary research. They spent three days and nights working in the cities of Araraquara, Rio Claro and Rio Preto, then returned to North America for the second major phase of the project.

That phase included checking in various parts of the martin's nesting range the following nesting season to see how many of these marked birds could be found. A team of licensed banders was lined up by Klimkiewicz's office to spot check colonies in various parts of the range. In addition, a range-wide appeal was made in the U.S. and Canada for persons to salvage wings from martins found dead and mail them to the bird banding lab in Laurel, Maryland.

When it was over, more than 1,500 martins had been checked and 31 marked martins identified. They didn't answer all the questions the program had gone after, but they did provide some very exciting information.

First, the bad news: Some of the colors proved very difficult to detect. Most of the 31 carried the most conspicuous of the five colors — fire orange — which had been applied in Barretos. The predominance of this color among the results led researchers to suspect that many other

Seeds for the ultraviolet migration project were sown when Dalgas Frisch and his wife, Birte, visited Purple Martin Junction in 1984. As a token of good will — and clear evidence that the Sao Paulo birds were indeed purple martins — his organization presented to the Nature Society a pair of purple martins that had been salvaged and mounted in Brazil. His tour of the Junction attracted the attention of the news media, who made much of the first-time meeting between martin authorities of two continents.

The team that checked quality of ultraviolet markings and did other background work on the migration project in early February, 1985, represented three organizations from two nations. From left to right, they included James R. Hill III of the Nature Society; Kathy Klimkiewicz of the U.S. Bird Banding Laboratory at Laurel, Maryland; Tom Coulson of the Nature Society; Connie Knittle; Birte Frisch; Ed Knittle of the Denver Wildlife Research Center; and Dalgas Frisch, vice president of the Brazilian Association for Preservation of Wildlife. This photo was taken at the Frisches' plantation, Fazenda Indaia, near Piracicaba in central Sao Paulo.

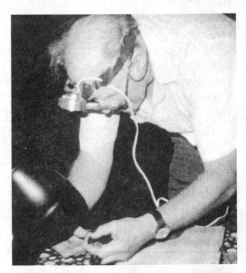

Terry Carter of Arlington Heights, Illinois, was one of the designated bird banders who spot-checked martin colonies in various parts of the range. Here he's shown checking the Purple Martin Junction colony, which proved to have no marked birds in it, much to our disappointment.

feathers had actually carried markings that simply could not be detected.

Some birds from each of the five cities were found, but the distribution of those from Barretos was the big story. Those 22 birds were located in places as scattered as central Alberta, the Niagara Falls and Chesapeake Bay areas, Kansas City, Dallas and New Orleans — a major part of the range.

Moreover, when all 31 are included, the recoveries extend as far east as Nova Scotia, indicating that birds from those five flocks in an area of central Sao Paulo are distributed throughout all the range east of the Rockies, with the possible exception of Florida and the southeastern states.

While the study did not prove anything about routes, it strongly suggested that all those in southern Brazil use the Mexican land route. And it clearly demonstrated there is much mixing of flocks during migration. Even though they come back home with a high degree of regularity, martins apparently are very cosmopolitan in their off-season activities.

In addition to the spraying, closer observation on the winter flocks themselves was initiated, both in Sao Paulo state and at various locations between there and central America.

Consequently, Frisch has developed a new theory about the route used by those southern Brazilian flocks. Because he has seen migrating flocks at several locations along this route, he believes they use a route that angles close to Bolivia and then moves north through the western Amazon basin, reaching the coast somewhere in the vicinity of Caracas, Venezuela, and then moving west and north along the coast of South America, Central America and Mexico.

If this is accurate, it still leaves major questions unanswered. Some martins winter in various locations in the Amazon and northern South America. Do they move into this pattern, or follow a completely different island route through the Caribbean?

And do all those southern Brazilian martins follow the Mexican route to completion, or do some split at Yucatan and fly directly across to Louisiana, or hop northeast to Cuba and Florida?

Or are the martins of Florida and the southeast a separate population that winters in the Amazon or even in the islands?

These questions remain, but we are getting much closer to the answers.

The progressive movement of the population during migration was clearly illustrated for the first time in 1986. On February 16, a day in which scouts had already been reported in 10 southern states as far north as Cape Girardeau, Missouri, and as far east as Siler City, North Carolina, Canadian author Andre Dion watched very large numbers at Maracaibo, Venezuela; Dalgas Frisch watched a flock of 30,000 at Caceres on the Paraguay River in southwestern Brazil; and Jamie Hill reported substantial numbers still at some of the winter sites in southern Brazil.

Dalgas Frisch and Luis Vizotto in early 1985 studied a large flock of purple martins at a refinery at Manaus in the central Amazon basin. Were these birds migrating from the wintering sites farther south, or were they part of a separate population that winters in the Amazon valley? Many questions remain to be answered before the complete migration picture is established.

Apparently, martins were strung out along the entire 5,000-mile route south of the U.S., plus a good part of the U.S. range as well.

Moreover, the ultraviolet experiment of the preceding year had strongly suggested that each of the many flocks contains birds from many areas — but the complete populations of no areas.

Nature thus prevents the population of any community from being wiped out by one of nature's own storms.

Dalgas Frisch, after observing flocks at several points along this route in 1985, believes this is the primary route used by martins. This route runs through the western Amazon basin, rather than the central basin, as formerly presumed. This one, however, cannot account for the large number of martins found at Manaus, and smaller numbers at other points farther east. And no clear evidence yet exists on how martins reach Florida.

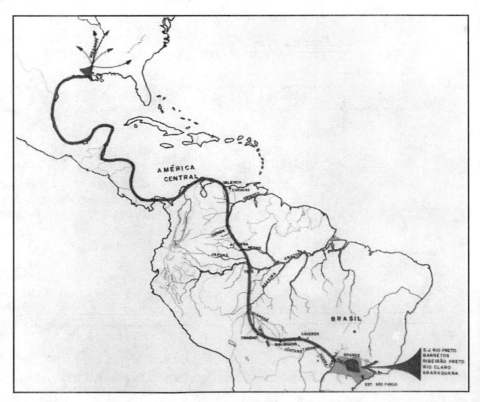

Martins seem attracted to plazas because they are well lighted. Some flocks have moved into these locations immediately after installation of bright mercury vapor lights, leading some observers, including Frisch, to believe these lights are the cause.

Wintering **flocks use utility wires to some extent, but most roost in trees — almost always in the upper 10-ft. layer of foliage.**

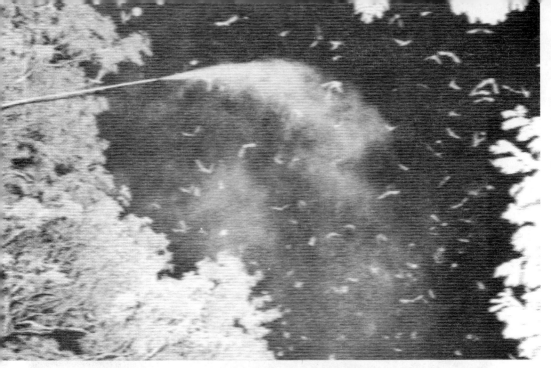

In late January, 1985, more than 250,000 purple martins were roused from their sleep in the middle of the night long enough to fly through a fine mist containing paint pigment visible only under ultraviolet light. The flocks were roosting in five cities and a different color was used for each flock. Most birds acquired only a few microdots of color. Engesa, a Brazilian military contractor, supplied equipment and personnel to assist the Brazilian Association for Preservation of Wildlife in completing the marking phase of that project.

The U.S. research team, assisted by Sao Paulo's Dr. Luis Vizotto (holding bamboo pole in foreground), netted several hundred birds late at night on that plaza and checked them for quality of marking. Individual martins were kept safe in net produce bags until they could be checked, after which they were released before dawn the next morning.

One of the flocks in the 1985 ultraviolet marking project roosted in this plaza in Sao Jose do Rio Preto, in northern Sao Paulo state. That flock of 70,000 roosted in 17 trees. At dawn each day, a municipal crew hosed the night's droppings off the central plaza. The birds left the plaza just before dawn each morning, and each evening assembled in the sky between 6:30-7 p.m. then in a period of six minutes descended into the trees and settled in for the night.

Brazilian wintering flocks often pack so closely together on branches that they create a weight problem for branches, even though each bird weighs only two ounces. This flock, photographed in 1984 in the state of Sao Paulo, shows only moderate density. Purple martins are often mixed with gray-breasted and brown-chested martins in these flocks — two species that stay behind when Progne subis comes home to North America.

Nesting Activities

The reproduction cycle typically is divided (very roughly) into three periods of a month each. The first involves pair-formation and nest-building. The second involves laying and brooding of eggs. The third involves feeding of young.

For early spring arrivals, a month may pass before this three-month cycle starts. And some may remain in an area a month after the young have fledged, so some martins remain in the nesting area five months of each year.

Those early arrivals often wait awhile for a very good reason — the possibility of bad weather. A martin can live 3-4 days without food, then it deteriorates rapidly and dies within another day or two. Cold snaps rarely last until that critical fourth day, however. Usually two days is the limit and all martins recover.

Nevertheless, martins are slow to begin nesting, having learned deep in their genes over thousands of years of survival that while they can save themselves during a few days of bad weather, they could not do so if their systems were already trying to produce eggs or feed young. Reproduction waits for warmer weather.

Late spring arrivals, on the other hand, waste little time.

Let's take a closer look at what occurs during this three-month period:

Older (ASY) birds often seem to be paired when they arrive. These are probably pairs from previous years since they do not mate in South America. Many older birds and all younger (SY) birds are not mated when they arrive.

Most ASY birds eventually mate and a majority of SY birds do, too, but a colony may have a substantial number of SY birds that do not succeed in mating.

The mating procedure usually starts with a male selecting a compartment and then trying to "sell" himself and that compartment as a package deal. When females are in the vicinity, the male increases his activity around the cavity — going in and out, flying out and returning to the house, diving into the entrance and so on. This activity seems to attract the female and stimulate her interest in that cavity.

The popular St. Louis naturalist, Otto Widman, described this process much more picturesquely than I can. In 1907 he wrote:

"The very early and really untimely return of the old martin in spring can only be explained by a strong desire to take possession of a suitable nesting site before others arrive. He knows that without a desirable home his chances for getting a spouse are slim. He knows that on her frail heart his glossy coat makes no impression if it is not backed by a comfortable home. His melodious and rapturous carols will attract her, but before she makes up her mind to stay she satisfies herself that the house he offers suits her ideas of a home and nursery.

"In possession of a box of his choice the old martin sticks to it and awaits the arrival of the females. Sometimes he has to wait for weeks, but whenever the weather is propitious his eyes scan the firmament, and as soon as he discovers the coveted object his voice is raised in ecstacy. A female thus attracted soon alights and the whole colony is in the greatest excitement, every male doing his best to invite the sweet newcomer into his house. After a little rest and meditation she settles daintily at the side of one of the noisy wooers, whose entreaties become still more boisterous. He persuades her into his house, but she only looks attentively into it at first. She may or she may not enter it. She reflects, is undecided, and goes off into the air, accompanied by an excited outcry from the whole colony. Immediately all males are at her side, and drawing beautiful circles around her bewitching form beseech her in the most passionate terms.

"Soon she returns, goes from one box to the other, comes back again and sits on neutral ground to reconsider the situation. The whole maneuver may not take more than half an hour and the choice is made. The rejected suitors content themselves immediately and fights are rare among old people who respect each other's domain, but after the arrival of the birds of the second year, when both females and vacant bird boxes become scarcer, quarrels are more numerous."

There's actually a little more to it than that. In a typical situation, males occasionally during the waiting period have to defend their chosen room or house against other males. When a female is investigating a room she may have to defend it against another female — even if she isn't sure yet that she wants it. During the pair formation process most of the fighting that breaks out involves males versus males and females versus females, but none of it is serious.

The bonding process itself occurs over a period of a few hours to a few days. For a few days the pair gradually shows increased awareness of each other and finally, without giving any unusual or ritualistic signs, they begin to act as a pair. They show excitement at seeing each other, even at a distance, and feed, preen and loaf together. They may not begin to build a nest together, however, for as long as three weeks.

Pair bonds are strongest in the morning. For a few days they tend to weaken as the day passes, and sometimes disintegrate in the evening. Usually, however, they are re-established and strengthened the next morning during the period of peak social activity in the colony.

Nest-building is often a casual affair, and may continue for as long as a month. At Purple Martin Junction, some building starts in late April, but the first period of intense activity is normally during the first week of May — about one month after those first resident birds arrived. After a few days, the intense activity tapers off, and thereafter is sporadic. Some SY birds can be seen carrying in nest materials in early June, but most nest-building occurs in May.

Allen and Nice called nest-building a "contagious activity," triggered by both warm temperatures and the nest-gathering activities of other martins.

Males often initiate the nest-building, but after a few days their enthusiasm wanes and the females take over the main responsibility. As the period progresses the males begin to court the females aggressively.

Sexual activity increases. Copulation occurs, usually in early morning, sometimes on the house and sometimes on the ground. Males sometimes have to defend their mates from other males, who become excited by the presence of a female in a receptive condition. Gang rapes do occur, but usually a male is able to drive other males away without undue difficulty.

Copulation ceases when egg-laying begins. Widmann described this phase of the cycle in this way:

"When the construction of the nest is nearing completion the happy couple visits the apple tree to line the nest with green leaves. The nest is now ready for the reception of eggs and oviposition begins. In strong contrast to the doings of the European house sparrow, which continually offends the eyesight by his endless attempts, the copulations of the martin are performed at such an early hour of the morning that they are seldom seen by human eyes. At this period, when in the dawn of the morning he greets the approaching day with sweet music from the door of his home, the voice of the male martin has a peculiar softness, and his utterances on these occasions are entirely different from what he says at other times."

EGG-LAYING AND INCUBATION

Among martins, most important events happen during the early morning, and egg-laying is no exception. Eggs are laid early in the morning on successive days. If the weather turns temporarily cooler, a hen may skip a day or two.

Incubation starts only when all eggs have been laid, so that all birds in the brood hatch at approximately the same time. This is true of most, but not all, species of birds.

Only the female incubates. She spends about three-fourths of each day on the eggs. During the remaining time while she is out feeding, the male guards the nest. If the weather becomes cooler than normal, she will spend more time on the eggs, running as high as 90 percent of the time.

Incubating, however, is not done in long periods. Typically, a female spends 10-15 minutes on the eggs and 5-10 minutes off. Again, cool weather may alter this, and cause her to stay on the eggs for a half-hour at a time, with only brief intervals away.

Even though eggs are brooded together, and hatch on the same day (or sometimes over a two-day period), they usually hatch in the order in which they were laid.

Most broods hatch in 15-16 days, although this may vary a day or so in either direction.

Occasionally nestlings of noticeably different ages occur in the same nest, and it's difficult to establish whether they have common parentage. Typically, the age difference is only a week or two, and I suspect the "dump nest" idea is the most likely answer — that the young eggs were put in the nest by another female who was confused about her nest and simply got into the wrong compartment each morning to lay her eggs.

In 1983, however, Denny Marcum of Hamilton, Ohio, watched a brood fledge from a compartment, and only two weeks later found newly hatched young in the same compartment. Those eggs had to have been laid while young were still being fed in the compartment, and it seems unlikely any neighboring mother would make that kind of mistake.

FEEDING

For the first few days after hatching the male does most of the feeding and the female stays in the nest and broods the young just as she did the eggs. Then she joins the feeding operation. Both parents work hard at this, although over the long haul the female probably does a little more than the male.

Many people have counted trips made by martins to feed young, and results are always impressive. Otto Widmann made one of the most notable such studies in 1884. He counted trips by 16 pairs during the period of 4 a.m. to 8 p.m.

In summarizing Widmann's study, Allen and Nice reported:

"The number of visits from 5 to 6 was 118, during the next hour 171, for the next six hours they totaled 202, 232, 276, 255, 217, 250; from 1:00 to 3:00 they dropped to 132 and 119 during a light rain; they reached their maximum — 459 — between 3:00 and 4:00, while the last four hours came to 224, 166, 195 and 177."

That's a total of 3,193 bugs and/or mouthfuls of bugs, or approximately 200 per pair. But that's just peanuts compared to what they are capable of. Apparently the rainy conditions on Widmann's test day kept activity down.

In 1983, Farmer Sergent of West Liberty, Kentucky, watched a single pair feeding four young for one hour, 9-10 a.m. Those two martins fed the young 86 times.

And also in 1983, John L. E. Coburn of Fayetteville, Arkansas, watched

Here's a martin exiting with a waste sac that had been deposited in the nest by a nestling. The sacs are carried a safe distance away to avoid fouling the nest and making it vulnerable to predators.

Purple martins drink and bathe on the wing and rarely use a birdbath in the manner of most songbirds. But it has happened, and James Stillman of Dolliver, Iowa, caught this pair in the act.

a lone female feeding a late brood in late August. "One day we watched her fly 18 times in less than 20 minutes about 50 feet from her house," Coburn wrote, "and each time caught an insect. She caught the insects almost in the same spot each time. We could see the insects in her beak."

That's almost one a minute.

WASTE SAC REMOVAL

Martins are one of many species who systematically remove waste from their nests. This is a defense mechanism to prevent nests from becoming smelly and attracting predators. In the case of martins, the parent birds regularly carry fecal waste sacs from the nest, usually as soon as the young have deposited them. Often on feeding trips they exchange food for feces, carrying something both ways.

We have seen parents carry sacs 100 yards or more, dropping them in a field across the highway from the Junction, but some observers who have made a point to study this claim the average distance is much less.

One of the more interesting observations that may relate to this was made some years ago by John Hoke, a resource manager for the National Park Service. In a study of Pawley's Island, South Carolina, which has many martin colonies, he noticed that vegetation was most lush within a 40-ft. radius of each house. Were martin droppings acting as effective fertilizer?

During the first two weeks of the nest period, parents are pretty zealous about keeping nests and houses clean. Then that dedication begins to break down and during the latter part of the period compartments become a little less than squeaky clean.

Nestlings soon learn to turn their posteriors toward the door and deposit their wastes outside or at least close to the door. This makes it easy for the older birds to pick up. But during the later part of the nest period, it also accounts for the fact that some waste build-up often occurs on porches just outside doors. Unless you let this accumulate from year to year, it should be easy to clean off at season's end, however.

RATE OF DEVELOPMENT

Typically, martins stay in the nest 28 days, more or less. Earliest we have seen young leave the nest and fly well is 22 days, but I suspect most that leave this early do not survive. A martin will not leave at this age unless frightened. At this age they are actually overweight and, although they have full plumage, have not developed their final flight configuration. Martins trim up considerably during their fourth week in the nest.

Here's a brief look at how they develop:

During their first week, nestlings are fed very small insects and crushed insects. As they grow older they are fed larger insects, and more often. Occasionally, insects as large as dragonflies are brought to the nest during the second and third week, even though the young cannot handle them. It is not until the fourth week that dragonflies and other large insects become common fare.

Widmann said that insects with stingers, such as bees and wasps, are never brought to the young. For that matter, they are rarely eaten by the older birds, either.

Small insects are often crushed together and brought home as a pellet — a much more efficient way of utilizing tiny food sources.

Nestlings grow very rapidly during their first two weeks and have achieved almost their maximum weight by that time. They add a little more weight until around their 20th day when they reach maximum weight. Then they lose weight during their final week in the nest.

Young nestlings carry a lot of excess fat during their second and third weeks, and this is probably used up in feather generation.

David B. Hibbett of Nashville is among those who have kept careful daily records of weight gains. In 1985, he studied a clutch of six which hatched June 5 and weighed three grams each when hatched. In August of that year, he wrote:

"On day 2, the average weight was 5.8 grams (a gain of 2.8 grams). On

day 3. . .8.7 grams (a gain of 2.9 grams). Day 4 shows a gain of 3.2 grams.
"The gain on day 5 was 3.7 grams and, in the days that followed, the acceleration soared! The 10th day shows an increase of 8.2 grams. the greatest single day increase during the entire brooding period!"

Hibbett's birds gained only around 2.0 grams per day from day 11 to 15, at which point they weighed 58 grams. This particular group reached its peak of 62.5 grams on day 19 and began to shrink. At their final weigh-in on day 27, their average weight was 53.3 grams.

One more interesting point in Hibbett's experiment is worth mentioning. Fearing that his daily handling could affect the daily gains of the birds, he left a "control" nest — a brood of young on the back side of the house that hatched the same day as his test group.

He weighed them only once, at the age of 23 days, and found they actually weighed seven grams less than the ones that were handled daily.

Robert Allen summarized the growth pattern this way: "One young purple martin weighed 2.8 grams directly after hatching. Individuals hatched early in the morning will weigh as much as four grams by nightfall. The little birds gain rapidly until 12 days of age, when they weigh from 42 to 47 grams. After this they gain less rapidly until about the 20th day when they weigh between 55 and 60 grams. They then begin to lose weight, and when they leave the nest at about the 28th day, they weigh between 47 and 52 grams."

Most feather growth occurs between the 12th and 20th days. Allen described feather development this way"

"Most newly hatched purple martins I have observed were entirely devoid of natal down. Two individuals possessed a few filaments. . .Both lost this down on the first or second day of nest life. At hatching the retrices and remiges can be seen beneath the skin and their tips protrude about 1/2 mm. The inside of the mouth is a pale yellow. The line that marks the eye slit can be seen high up on he eyeball. A small egg tooth is present.

"The 2nd day the birds are little changed except for increase in weight, but the dorsal feather tract can be seen through the skin. From the 3rd to the 6th day the bird increases in weight and becomes more active in righting itself when overturned. The eye slit deepens and on the 6th day the eye can be opened, although it is usually kept closed. The feather tracts gradually appear under the skin and become darker in color.

"From the 7th to the 11th day the bird continues to increase in weight, but still remains inactive. The feeding reaction can be obtained most easily when the birds are about eight days old. About the 9th day the eyes are kept open to some extent and by the 11th day most of the time. The skin, which was at first flesh colored, becomes dull blue because of the feathers developing beneath it; as yet the feathers have not begun to emerge from the skin.

"From the 12th to the 20th day the bird grows a large part of its coat of

Daily growth pattern

This 27-day sequence by Tom Dellinger of Duncanville, Texas, shows typical development of nestlings. Dellinger used photos from two different broods in the sequence, but all ages are correct. The coins used for size comparisons are quarters. "By four days," he wrote, "tiny black feathers are forming under the skin. By six days, the original pink color is now turning dark from the pin feathers under the skin. By nine days, the pin feathers are through the skin on the wings and tail. By the 13th day, the feathers all over the body are out of the pin cases. By 17 days, the baby is covered with feathers but with pin cases remaining near the body. By 20 days the feathers have flattened out. . ."

1

2

3

4

5

6

7

8

9

10

11

12

13

14

15

16

17

18

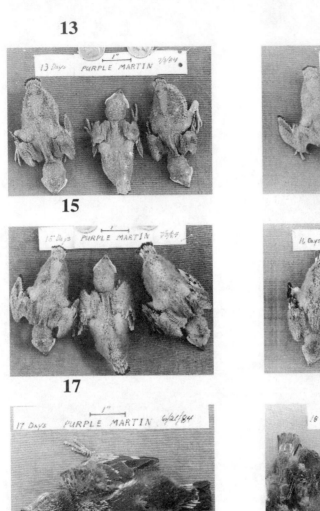

19

20

21

22

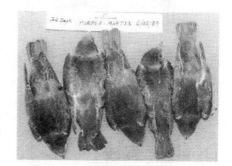

23

24

25

26

27

feathers. The retrices and remiges are the first to begin this rapid growth. The 6th primary increases from 4 to 70 mm. during this period. Retrices and remiges start losing their sheaths about the 14th day and on the 20th only a small sheath remains around the bases of these feathers. On the 14th and 15th days the rest of the feather tracts begin their rapid growth and by the 20th day this is largely completed."

Allen also recorded the development of reactions. He noted that even a day-old nestling could be stimulated to lift its head and cheep weakly to beg for food, but only once during any general period unless it was fed. About their reactions he wrote:

"The first appearance of fear reactions occurs on the 14th or 15th day. At this time the birds will crowd to the back of the room and remain very quiet when in danger. If picked up they will struggle and peck at the hand that holds them. Even after being placed on the ground they will remain perfectly quiet until disturbed again, when they may try to escape by running over the ground. As they grow older they lose the tendency to remain quiet and will attempt to find a place to hide when set down. Later they will not stay in the room when frightened, but will attempt to fly long before they are capable of doing so successfully. On the 15th or 16th day they will return to the room if placed on the porch in front of it.

"From the 21st to 28th days the birds lose weight while completing the growth of their flight feathers. It is essential for them to be able to fly when they leave the nest and to be able to return to the same spot where their parents fed them, as the adult birds will not feed their young on the ground."

That last statement is not universally true, but nearly so. We've had reliable reports of parents who fed young on the ground, but we haven't been able to get one to do it. I've picked up grounded young and set them on a sparrow trap only three feet above the ground, and watched the parents promptly begin feeding; then put the young back on the ground, whereupon the feeding stopped.

That's a reaction we don't understand — there really seems no reason for it because martins do alight on the ground at times. But that's not more curious than the fact martins will pick up grit on a bird feeder but will die before they can recognize insect food on a feeder in cold weather.

FLEDGING

What happens to young martins during the time between fledging and the start of migration to Brazil?

Most martin enthusiasts know that, in general, martins spend progressively more time away from the houses as the young lose their dependence on it, and within a week or two abandon the house altogether. It's often difficult to keep track of exactly what each family in a colony is doing, and even when a person can do this he finds all sorts of variations occurring on this theme.

But there does appear to be a more or less standard pattern on which these variations are based. The most interesting and useful account of this post-fledgling period that I've seen was published a few years ago by Charles R. Brown, then of Sherman, Texas. Although Brown now has a doctoral degree and is on the staff of Yale University, he did this study in the 70s while still in school.

In "Post-Fledging Behavior of Purple Martins," published in the Wilson Bulletin (90(3), 1978, pp. 376-385), he traced in detail the activities of 26 broods during the week or so following fledging. He made general studies in north-central Texas during the years 1974-77, including detailed studies in 1974 and 1975. During those two years he kept close tabs on 26 broods, most of them for at least 4-5 days after fledging.

He found that broods were probably independent by 7-10 days, but definitely stayed together 4-5 days, the first 2-3 of these at a "grouping area." Each brood had its own grouping area, usually within a one-kilometer radius of the martin house, but rarely within a direct line of sight of that house or any other martin house.

Reason for isolating a grouping area from any martin house was to avoid attracting attention of "raiders," vagrant adult martins that harass any new young birds in their neighborhoods. Brown noted these raiders harassed young birds, whether on the porch of a house before fledging, in the air after fledging, or on wires in grouping areas. In the air they tried to force the young bird to the ground. Other times they tried to pull the young bird off porches or wires. Brown noted such harassment rarely resulted in injury, and may have a valuable function in increasing a young bird's survival reactions.

He found that even though birds in a brood usually did not fledge the same day (broods of six often fledged over a three-day period), the parents were able to reassemble the family each day. A key to this was a "choo choo" call uttered frequently by the young, and apparently recognizable to the parents.

Even though parents apparently could not recognize their own young by sight from others of the same age, they were remarkably successful in keeping their broods together. An occasional bird was lost from its own brood and adopted by another but, by and large, the broods stayed intact.

Survival rate among the 26 broods he studied was nearly 100 percent during those post-fledging days. He attributed this to numerous factors. Among them were the practice of fledging while a parent was present, which minimized lost birds; the "choo choo" sound which helped broods stay together; the practice of perching on exposed wires which also helped parents notice them; the practice of returning to the house at night or during storms; and various aspects of the parents' close attention and feeding activity.

Brown even concluded that the habit of raiders pursuing and attacking fledglings may have advantages. He noticed this makes it very difficult for a young bird to alight, and staying off the ground is almost essential to survival of a fledgling during its first few days.

As young approached fledging age, they usually came out on porches 1-4 days before fledging. They sat, flapped their wings, and were fed on the porches.

Although various observers have reported parents pulling young off the porches to get them to fly, Brown never saw this happen. When a young bird was pulled from a porch, it was always done by a raider while the parents were away. More often, the young bird got away and retreated back inside the nest cavity. When the parents returned, they always chased these raiders away.

When the young did leave it was usually in the morning, and they almost always followed a parent directly as it left the house. When the young bird was established on a wire or antenna somewhere away from the colony, the parent returned to the colony, often to lead another young one from the house.

The parents continued to feed the young in the grouping area, bringing them dragonflies and other large insects. They would first land on the wire beside the young to transfer food, then by the third day would hover in front of the young bird for the transfer. Gradually the young bird would become more aggressive, reaching out and grabbing the insect away from the parent.

By the fourth day, the birds made in-flight transfers. As parents approached with food, young would fly out to meet them. Sometimes the juvenile seized the food directly. Sometimes the parent dropped it, and if the juvenile failed to catch it, the parent would catch it before it reached the ground and repeat the process.

Brown was not able to determine when the parents stopped feeding the young, but confirmed they continued during the 4-5 days he followed the typical brood. He did see young birds begin to pursue and catch insects by themselves on the fourth and fifth day out of the nest.

Parents with their young usually returned to the colony house each night. On six occasions they returned in the daytime during storms but left soon after the storm passed. Parents began to return regularly during the daytime from 7-10 days after fledging, and Brown concluded the young may have been independent by then.

Both male and female parents were very active in feeding and defending the young in the grouping areas, but it was usually the female that led them back to the house each night. Although Brown did not always learn where the broods went each day after leaving the grouping area, he noted they remained near because they continued to return to the house each night.

J. Paul Perron of St. Jean, Quebec, sent these photos to the Nature Society News. The first shows a food "pellet" after it accidentally fell from a martin's mouth. The second shows it disassembled to reveal nearly two dozen caddis flies that were being brought home to the nestlings.

On one occasion he did manage to relocate a brood after it had left its grouping area. About that, he wrote:

"In 1974 one brood remained at the grouping area for five days. On the sixth day I found this brood grouped on wires along a rural road 2.1 km from their grouping area. This new area was largely open with cultivated fields predominant. I saw other broods in that area, and the juveniles were mingling freely. I suspect that other broods had also arrived there after leaving their grouping areas."

SECOND BROOD BEHAVIOR

Many of the parents that returned to the house during the day after the young had become independent then began to show nest-defense behavior, just as they did in early spring prior to breeding. They did not go through with the breeding cycle, of course, but Brown has reported rare cases in which martins have gone ahead and raised second broods.

During the past two decades we have had other reliable reports of this happening, too, almost always in the south where the season is longer.

For example, Steven Kroencke, then at Havana, Florida, reported in 1972, ". . .the biggest surprise of all — one pair raised two broods. I'm completely sure of this. Their first young left the nest during the second week of May. At first this pair would bring their babies back to sleep in their gourd. During the day the male would carry green leaves to his nest and chase away first-year males. Their second brood left the nest during the second week of July."

Mary and Ralph Schilling reported a case even father south, at McAllen, Texas, in 1984. Their scouts arrived February 9 that year and nesting started at a normal time, but their last birds departed on August 12, a late date for them. That's because one pair raised two broods.

After fledging the first brood of five, they had laid four new eggs by June 24 and by July 8 had four more young in the nest. Only two survived — one fledged August 3 and the other August 5.

One of our rare non-southern reports was also one of the most unusual. In this case, Mable Stewart of Kansas City, Missouri, watched two pairs each lay seven eggs, hatch and fledge six each, and then build second nests and lay second clutches. Each hatched a second brood of five and fed them for the normal time, although she is not certain how many fledged successfully. If they all flew, these two pairs produced a total of 22 young that season (1973) and that's probably some kind of record.

Late fledglings usually fly in time to migrate. Even if a bird fledges in late August in the midwest after its own flock has departed the immediate area, other flocks from farther north will be moving through in September.

Occasionally we hear of a bird that doesn't make it, however, and we have had a few cases where hand-raised birds eventually spent the winter with the person who raised them. Rose Minda's probably stayed around the longest, however.

Rose Minda of Avella, Pennsylvania, saved a bird from her brother-in-law's colony when it was devastated by Hurricane Agnes in 1972. She raised it. . .and it refused to leave her, stayed with her that winter, and the next, and the next. When released, the bird refused to wander far from its home base, or to join other martins, or to migrate. Each fall she took it in again. At last report, the bird had been with her nine years.

Chapter 7

The Purple Martin's Range

In the world of North American birds, the 100th principal meridian — which forms the east boundary of the Texas panhandle and extends on north through the Great Plains — is the traditional dividing line between eastern and western species. The 100th meridian doesn't indicate where martins cease to nest, however, just where confusion sets in.

In fact, martins can be found in most of the western states, but only in the northwestern coastal regions can they be attracted to houses with reasonable success. Western martins are a special case. For reasons of convenience, I am going to talk about martins in the western states in chapter 8. In this chapter, I will deal with those martins east of the Rockies, all of which will nest in houses.

In defining the limits of the martin's range east of the Rockies, let's start in west Texas and work our way clockwise around the range until we reach southern Florida, then finish with a few special notes.

In Texas, martins are common in parts of the dry west, but we have very few reports west of the Odessa-Midland area. El Paso is apparently out of the range. We do have a few reports of active colonies in New Mexico, but believe very few nest there and, in fact, those that do may be western martins, of the subspecies Progne subis hesperia, explained in chapter 8. They nest in single compartment houses, but that may be because multiple compartment houses have not been tried there in any numbers.

Martins are attractable throughout most of the Great Plains states, but become very scarce in the high plains, those huge flat eastern expanses of Colorado, Wyoming and adjoining parts of other states.

Numerous colonies, for example, exist in St. Francis, Kansas, practically on the Colorado border, but we have never had a report of an active colony in the Colorado plains.

Dr. A. M. Bailey, who authored "Birds of Colorado," described the martin there as, ". . .a rare summer resident and local breeder in western counties. . .While there are a few records of martins observed in western Colorado, all of the reports of nesting seem to be from the eastern part of the state."

Our experience echoes that observation.

In regard to the western slope, where the martins in question may actually be western martins, the late Howard Caudle, a resident of Grand

Junction, undertook to locate the martin colonies in that area. In June, 1968, he wrote:

"I have talked to a few old timers who came from the east to settle here many years ago. They all agreed there were many martins along the Colorado River in the years when Glenwood Springs, Rifle, Grand Junction, Colorado, and Moab, Utah, were first settled. . .

"I have been informed that scouts still pass through this valley each spring, but move on to prepared nesting places. If so, colonies do not return through in the autumn."

In November, 1969, Mr. Caudle added:

"Mr. Glen Rogers of the Colorado Department of Game, Fish and Parks informed me last May that a purple martin hit his car, killing the bird. Mr. Rogers brought the dead bird in for study.

"The Dale Lukes out in the county placed one large martin house in their yard. The purple martins came, but remained only for one day. . .

"Two weeks ago while walking my dog on the Indian Wash, I passed a home with a bird house made for 12 pairs. On stopping and talking to the lady of the house, this lady informed me that purple martins had nested successfully for several years, but due to the fact that she was unable to clean the house last spring, the sparrows took over. . ."

In Cortez, in the southwestern part of the state, nature enthusiasts who had discovered martins nesting in a house in that area investigated the possibility of attracting martins to help with mosquito control. We did not feel their chances of immediate success were very great and said so, but encouraged them to make an effort to see if the population could be built up in that area. We don't think the project developed beyond that point, however.

From Laramie, Wyoming, Furcel F. Friday wrote in 1972, "Last year we had a pair of purple martins and they had two little ones. We thought we would have more this year, but our pair this year keeps chasing away any other purple martins that appear."

That's the only report of an active nest in a house that we have from Wyoming. Obviously, there are others, but the Jaycees of Saratoga tried in the 1960s to start martins in that southern Wyoming community, and got only tree swallows in the houses.

The situation is much the same in Montana, where there are old records of both sightings and colonies, but none in our currently active files. I suspect if active colonies do exist they are in the Missouri Valley in the eastern part of the state.

Martins are rather scarce around Calgary and points south, but become relatively common at Red Deer about halfway between Calgary and Edmonton. One of the 31 ultraviolet recoveries in 1985 was at Stettler, in that general area (it was marked at Barretos).

Martins are common in the Edmonton area, and the book, "The Birds of Alberta," by Salt Wilk, says they have nested as far north as Fort Mc-

Murray and the Peace River districts — 500 miles north of the international border. Even at far northern latitudes the Canadian lake regions have appeal for martins.

The Bent study lists casual records as far north as Whitemud River and Fort McMurray. And we have had references to martins apparently seen on Great Slave Lake in the southern part of the Northwest Territories.

Several years ago, one of our News readers, Helene R. White, maintained a colony at Rochester, about 80 miles north of Edmonton.

But the most extensive current information on that area is possessed by Joy and Cam Finlay of Edmonton. In 1985, they reported in the Edmonton Journal:

"The most northern. . .colony to be reported is at Winagami Provincial Park, north of High Prairie and west of Lesser Slave Lake. Stefan Jungkind found a purple martin in a man-made birdhouse at this park during his breeding bird survey. This is much farther north than our own colony on Thunder Lake, west of Barrhead, which was previously the most northern one known."

Winagami is about 180 miles northwest of Edmonton. Barrhead is about 60 miles northwest of Edmonton.

Martins have nested in tree cavities in that area, still do, even as far north as Lesser Slave Lake, but man-made housing is a fairly recent development. The Finlays traced that development:

"Among the first purple martin apartment houses in Alberta were those erected in Camrose in 1918, Red Deer around 1920, Elk Island National Park in 1937 and Kavanagh in 1939.

"The Edmonton population began when Mrs. M. Fisher put up a box near the University of Alberta in 1935 and three birds investigated. . .in 1937, a pair built a nest and laid six eggs in her box. The eggs were then destroyed by a wren! It took nine more years before martins were again reported to nest in Edmonton.

"In 1946 a pair appeared in the Fisher yard to successfully raise young. A second pair nested in a house erected by A. Allan in the north end the same season. The first nesting record in Calgary was in 1971, with starlings breaking the eggs.

"The Edmonton population built up to about 1,000 pairs by the early 1960s when we attracted the first pair to nest in the Fulton Place/Hardisty district. Within three years we had over 20 pairs. . .and then a neighbor shot most of them!

"By the late 1970s martin numbers within the city began to fall while increasing in Sherwood Park and acreages to the east. Today there are probably no more than a couple hundred pairs in the city but many nest in man-made houses to the east and south of Edmonton."

Edmonton, with a population in the neighborhood of a half-million, is the northernmost major city in North America. A casual glance at the continental map may cause some persons to puzzle over why either humans or martins would be plentiful that far north, but there are good reasons.

Edmonton lies in a rich, lake-dotted prairie, still temperate enough to be an important agricultural area, and that prairie is underlain with oil. In addition to oil and agriculture, Edmonton is an administrative center for the incomprehensibly vast section of the continent still farther north.

Although Edmonton lies 350 miles north of Montana and more than 1,000 miles north of Denver, it is almost as close to the Gulf of Mexico as it is to the Arctic Ocean.

The MacKenzie River, which is almost as long as the Mississippi, flows north to the Arctic Ocean — and it starts north of Edmonton. Approximately one-third of our continent lies north of Alberta, and is barely inhabited.

But central Alberta is another story. It is hospitable to man and martin alike. Margaret E. Wright of Halton Hills, Ontario, after a trip through Alberta, wrote, "What a wonderful country this is. . .Everywhere we went we saw purple martins flying around, even in Edmonton. . ."

Moving east, the range passes through the other prairie provinces of Saskatchewan and Manitoba. Bruce Cameron of Saskatoon reported many martins at Lake Wakaw, about 80 miles northeast of Saskatoon and 400 miles north of the international border. That is our northernmost report in that province.

In Manitoba, martins nest at least as far north as the 52nd Parallel, 250 miles north of the border. In 1973, J. S. Puls of Dauphin reported martins flourishing in the lake region known as the "Waterhen" district directly north of Brandon, and listed one of the largest colonies in Manitoba existing on the north shore of Lake Manitoba — a total of nearly 500 birds there by season's end.

David R. M. Hatch of the Manitoba Museum of Man and Nature in Winnipeg wrote that martins could still be found nesting in woodpecker holes in trees and utility poles in some parts of Manitoba.

And one of the most active bird clubs in North America is located there — The Manitoba Purple Martin Club.

We've had very few reports from the region of Ontario north of the Great Lakes, but we have few members there. We don't know how far north the range extends but do know that martins nest along the north shore — places like Thunder Bay, for example — we just don't now how common they are.

Likewise, we have a number of reports of active colonies along the northeast shore of Lake Huron, including rather sizable colonies in the Georgian Bay area, but don't know how common they are.

At Pembroke, Ontario, 75 miles northwest of Ottawa on the Ottawa River is a major swallow roost each August. More than 115,000 swallows, including martins, gather there each year, but according to the Pembroke Area Bird Club, most of them are usually barn, tree and bank swallows.

Arnold Froom, one of our most dedicated martin enthusiasts of Ottawa, is one who believes the longer hours of daylight in Canada are important to growing birds. In one of his letters to the Society, he remarked:

"I was born on a farm near the St. Lawrence River at the 45th Parallel exactly midway between the Equator and the North Pole. There are hundreds of martin houses in the Ottawa and St. Lawrence River valleys, and I think I have visited nearly every one. This is a good area for martins. In June, we have 16 hours of daylight and only eight hours of darkness. The parents have two hours for feeding the little ones for every hour of sleeping time. The babies grow rapidly and soon are taking flying lessons in preparation for the long hike to the Amazon Valley."

Wray Brand of Cardiff, Ontario, wrote, "Our location is about 100 air miles northeast of Toronto but we do have purple martins. Some here have their houses full."

From the Pembroke area the northern limit runs eastward somewhere north of the St. Lawrence, but we don't know where. We do know it extends north and northeast of Quebec City. Some years ago, Napoleon Beaudet reported colonies in Quebec City, Ville Vanier and St. Redempteur; and at Chateau Richer near the Isle of Orleans. The easternmost colony he knew about was at Ste. Anne de la Pocatiere, on the south shore of the St. Lawrence, 100 miles northeast of Quebec City. In that community, Rev. Rene Tanguay, who was in charge of a museum, also maintained a colony of martins.

From there, the range appears to extend east across the northern tip of Maine and then angle southeastward across central New Brunswick. We've had reports from Presque Isle in northern Maine, and presume they nest at least as far north as the northern tip.

Finland Dumond of Fort Kent has spent a lot of years trying to attract martins at that northern tip. He says they are there, alright, but scarce and hard to attract. He said two or three sightings per year are reported, but the nearest dependable nestings are around Presque Isle, 60 miles south.

Charles W. Horne of Milo gave us a better picture of martins in the center of Maine: ". . .about seven years ago a friend of mine erected a wooden house and has since added two aluminum houses, and he has a colony started. Two years ago he had about 18 pairs. . .I have put up two aluminum houses and have had one pair nest. . .Within a radius of 40 miles I know of several colonies, all hale and hearty. . .On the 15th of September, 1976, I stood in my backyard and counted over 500 martins that had gathered in two California poplars. . ."

Possibly the most thorough survey of martins in a large area was that of New Brunswick by Roy Hunter, whose information was accumulated during 1963-66 and published in 1967.

PURPLE MARTINS
IN
NEW BRUNSWICK
1966

WOODSTOCK

MONCTON

FREDERICTON

SUSSEX

ST. STEPHEN

LANCASTER   SAINT JOHN

● PURPLE MARTIN COLONY
○ MARTIN HOUSES UNOCCUPIED
● LARGEST COLONY
● 2ND LARGEST COLONY
● 3RD LARGEST COLONY

In 1967, during Canada's Centennial celebration, the late naturalist Roy Hunter of Moncton, surveyed martin colonies in New Brunswick. This map was published in his booklet, "A Centennial Survey of Purple Martins in New Brunswick." It provides an interesting look at the population in an area at the extreme northeast end of the range.

In that province at the extreme northeastern end of the range, Hunter located 66 active colonies and 29 unoccupied houses, most in a state of disrepair. Virtually all of the suitable houses were occupied, with some of them so full that "spill-over" martins were nesting in nearby tree swallow houses and miscellaneous cavities.

Most of the colonies were along the St. John and Petitcodiac rivers, a few on the eastern coast. Northernmost was that of Franklin Hickling at Florenceville in west-central New Brunswick near Maine. Easternmost was at West Brule on the coast.

Largest was that of Walter LeRoy Sharpe of Fredericton. He had nine houses, ranging in size from 6-9 compartments, all houses well occupied.

Oldest colonies were in Sunbury County in south-central New Brunswick. One was said to be more than 100 years old. Earliest ornithological reference to martins in New Brunswick is to a Point du Chene colony in 1883 in Brewster's writings.

Largest concentration was in the Geary area where eight houses in a fairly close area hosted a total of around 620 mature birds.

The only natural nesting sites he discovered were in a pair of trees on opposite sides of the St. John River near Camp Medley. These trees were riddled with woodpecker holes, and had fallen during a hurricane.

A familiar theme reoccurred frequently in Roy Hunter's study: Invariably, where houses had been neglected, starlings and house sparrows had taken over and they no longer were occupied by martins. This was true at a colony he investigated at Boiestown, in central New Brunswick, which he had heard was the northernmost inland colony. It may also have been the reason he found no martins nearly as far north as Chatham on the northeastern coast, which was listed in the range in the book, "Birds of New Brunswick."

Although our organization has no active records in either Nova Scotia or Prince Edward Island, some do exist there. In 1976, Mary Dievler, an experienced birder from Bradenton, Florida (formerly of Pennsylvania), observed martins in both areas during a tour of the Maritime Provinces.

In Hunter's survey, he found only one active colony, and that was at Amherst, just across the border from New Brunswick. At about the same time, Robie Tufts of Wolfville, author of "Birds of Nova Scotia," wrote that the martin was practically extirpated from that peninsular province, but did not know why. The only colony he cited was at Windsor, about 30 miles from Halifax.

Ironically, one of the 31 birds recovered in 1985 during the ultraviolet migration project was found at Oxford, Nova Scotia.

I don't know just how common purple martins once were in New England, but they were more common than they are now. They declined for a number of reasons.

The low coastal areas best suited to martins were among the first in North America to be heavily urbanized and industrialized, and that cut into their nesting sites. Then the house sparrow was established first in New England, and the effects of both sparrows and starlings were felt first in that area. Finally, New England weather is sometimes more severe in spring than in other parts of the range. Several cold late springs during the past century set the population back, and because of the other factors mentioned here, it has had difficulty recovering.

The spring most often mentioned is that of 1903. This note that appeared in The Auk in October, 1903, illustrates the problem:

"Mortality of Purple Martins [Progne purpurea] at Brattleboro, Vt. — during the long rain in June, 1903, the nests in the bird house belonging to William C. Horton of Brattleboro, Vt., became completely water-soaked, and thirty young and two adult purple martins were found dead in their nests. The remaining members of the martin colony abandoned the house, leaving twelve eggs unhatched. Occasionally a few return and fly about as if trying to catch a glimpse of the inside of their home but none have ventured to enter up to this date (July 17). — Frances B. Horton, Brattleboro, Vt."

This report is from the interior of New England, and this may be appropriate because the effects of weather may be especially critical to the interior, highland regions. I feel it is surely easier for the population to recover in the coastal regions, and this is apparently borne out by the fact that most of the colonies we know about are within 50 miles of the coast.

Those that are in the interior tend to favor river and lake areas. Columnist Stacey Cole of the Manchester Union-Leader, wrote, "Purple martins are not very common in New Hampshire. The largest colony I know about is at Funspot at Meredith." Meredith is on Lake Winnipesaukee in the south-central part of the state.

Martins are fairly common in western Vermont, especially in the Lake Champlain area, but we have few records in other parts of the Vermont-New Hampshire-northern Massachusetts area.

Perhaps the largest colony in all of New England was one at which the landlord waited 30 years to attract his first martin. Reginald Maxim of Middleboro, Massachusetts, finally attracted his first martin in 1956, and eventually built up a colony of around 150 pairs, using eight wooden houses and one aluminum house. (Maxim, who had operated a dairy farm, retired some years ago and moved from that location, and I do not know the current status of this colony.)

Middleboro is in southeastern Massachusetts.

Easiest way to get acquainted with martins in that region is to visit Plum Island Wildlife Refuge (I presume this colony is still active) in the Boston area. For quite a few years there has been a colony there, and a blind was erected so that visitors can watch their activities. Refuge personnel may also be able to list other colonies in that area.

In 1968, George H. Gormley of Warwick, Rhode Island, wrote: "I wonder if you have any information on the location of martins in Rhode Island." (We didn't have much.) "I know where most of them are on this side of Narragansett Bay. They — all two of them — seem to be clustered in the South County area within 10 miles of the ocean! Both colonies have about 30 birds each. . .Unfortunately, I am located about 20 miles north of the "PM Capital of RI." I expect I will have a VERY, VERY long wait before I attract a wandering pair."

But in another letter the following season, Gormley's impressions had changed somewhat — much to his delight.

"In my brief and very incomplete survey (which I am continuing this year) I located colonies with a total of about 400 adults. The discouraging part. . .that all these colonies are located within 10 miles of the southern shore of RI; there is none in my area in mid-state, and I had never seen a martin in this area. . .

"So things looked pretty bleak. . .But before I left (recently) I erected, quickly, another house. . .about 10 feet from the one-year-old wooden one.

"I returned from Ohio last week, June 14, and to my literal and utter disbelief, there were three martins sitting on the Trio house. . .I know now that I have a pair and a 'half,' the adult male had a mate and they are incubating eggs. . .and a young, 'bachelor' male who tries diligently during every one of the daylight hours to attract other martins to the house.

"Not only did I think I would never attract a colony, but I also doubted that there were even any birds anywhere near this area. The activities of this young male disprove that. He sometimes attracts two or three other martins daily. Perhaps these are young late-comers going to one of the large colonies in Massachusetts, Maine or even New Brunswick. From his activity, I get an idea of just how heavy the traffic in martins can be through an area where it is thought there are none!"

Carroll Quesnell of West Haven, Connecticut, noted the relative scarcity of martins there when he wrote in 1974, "I am amazed that the people in Connecticut don't know about martins. I have traveled all over the state looking for martins and so far have found only two colonies. One colony is about 40 miles from West Haven in New Milford and the other is in Branford, about 15 miles away. Both colonies have about 100 each."

Finally, on Long Island, colonies exist in numerous locations along the

With the exception of Fire Island and Brooklyn, martin colonies have been reported in all of the islands and communities named on this map. While this is by no means a complete list of colonies on the island, it suggests that the farther south and east a person lives the better are chances of attracting martins.

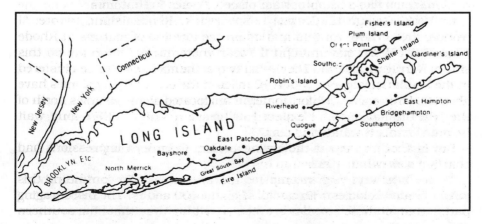

southern and eastern shores, but seem virtually non-existent in much of the western two-thirds, which is heavily populated with people. Urbanization and at least a temporary lack of interest may be the problem.

In the entire New York City metropolitan area, martins are scarce. We've had a few reports over the years, but only one large colony, and that was at Lemon Creek on Staten Island, which isn't exactly a metropolitan core area.

Colonies are also rather scarce in the dense central areas of Chicago, Detroit, Philadelphia and other very large cities. Even though martins are rather easy to attract along lake and riverfront areas, few efforts have been made even there. Life may be too intense in these central areas for people to have given much thought to cultivating something as low key and introspective as a purple martin colony.

There is one other area in which martins are strangely absent and that includes the Keys and a very small part of the southern tip of Florida. They have been seen migrating through that area, but do not nest there.

MEXICAN MIX UNCLEAR

The nesting range of the purple martin does extend well down into Mexico. In "Birds of Mexico," Emmet Blake said it breeds mainly on the central plateau, at least as far south as Guanajuato, which is about 150 miles northwest of Mexico City. It overlaps with the nesting range of the gray-breasted martin in the states of Tamaulipas, Coahuila and adjoining areas in eastern Mexico.

The breeding range of the western martin also extends down into western Mexico, and the exact limits of the three species and subspecies are not very clear to me. Perhaps a more careful delineation of these three ranges is a good project for some future date.

GRAY-BREASTED MARTINS

This seems like an appropriate place to enter a few comments on the gray-breasted martin, a look-alike species to the female purple martin. This species, whose range starts in Mexico and extends all the way into Argentina, often crops up in purple martin literature. This is the species with which the great wintering purple martin flocks of Brazil were confused for many years.

Over the years we've had a number of reports from Society members scattered from Oklahoma to Georgia who suspected they had seen gray-breasted martins. That isn't likely.

Kay McCracken, one of the most experienced birders in the Texas Gulf coast area, wrote in 1982:

"There they were — gray-breasted martins, at last. We had been birding a week in a southern Tamaulipas cloud forest and now by mid-morning had descended to the lowlands and a paved highway that should get us back to Brownsville, Texas, by nightfall. . .For gray-breasted martins, hawking the village plaza, we had to stop. . .Although these tropical cousins of our purple martin had been reported in Texas — usually erroneously — they are not really expected any nearer than that point (southern Tamaulipas).

"There are only two authenticated records of this species north of the Rio Grande, both in the previous century and both barely across the river.

"Though a bit smaller than purples, gray-breasts resemble them plumage-wise. Males are steely blue-black above, but never dark purple below. Both sexes resemble the female purple martin; cheeks, throat, breast and sides are grayish brown or dusky and the abdomen is nearly white. Females have some brown mixes with purplish above and both sexes have dark foreheads, not grayish like those of the female purple.

"Purple martins also breed in northern Mexico, but mostly up on the central plateau; gray-breasts are much more numerous, but rather keep to the lowlands, rarely living above 4,000 feet elevation. . .

"Gray-breasteds are as much attracted to human habitations as are our purple martins. Their habits, graceful flight, and twittering voices are also much alike though they take to nest boxes when provided, they more often build nests under eaves of buildings, in open church spires, or other cozy nooks. Saturday night band concerts in the village plazas seem not to bother the martin colonies nearby at all. Maybe they enjoy the music.

"Austin, in 'Birds of the World' tells of a pair in Guyana that lived in a box attached to the taffrail of a small river steamer, staying faithfully with the boat on its weekly 180-mile round trips up and down the river and successfully rearing brood after brood.

"Those in the northern part of their range are migratory and, like purple martins, return year after year to the same area, often to the same nest site."

ENVIRONMENTAL FACTORS

So now you know where martins can be attracted. Anywhere within the limits of at least the U.S. and Canadian range we have outlined here, you should be able to attract them. Inside this range, limiting factors become strictly local ones. For example, if your entire yard is covered by tree canopy, you won't attract martins.

If a neighboring factory spews smoke or otherwise fouls the air you may not attract them (we're still not sure of just what they will accept and what they won't). If you're in the middle of a desert miles from water you probably won't have much luck. And obviously there are other factors that influence their nesting choices that we don't know about, because no one can yet predict success with 100 percent certainty.

But anyone within the martin's range who has a suitable open area in his yard and erects a properly designed house has a reasonable chance of attracting them.

Chapter 8

Western Martins

Part of this chapter probably should have been included in my regular chapters on the purple martin, but for reasons of convenience I have continued to lump all martins found in the west as "western martins."

For years all martins west of the Rockies were considered a little different and lumped together as a subspecies, Progne subis hesperia, better known as western martins.

Many ornithologists now feel a difference exists between martins in the northwest and those in the southwest. They feel those in the northwest are, in fact, identical to those in the east, while some of those in the southwest are the only ones that should be classified as P. s. hesperia. This agrees with our impressions.

Martins of either type are not as common in the west as those in the east. Most active reports are from the coastal regions of British Columbia, Washington, Oregon, California; southern California and Arizona; and northwestern Mexico. They vary from rare to non-existent in vast areas of the great dry basin extending from the Rockies to the eastern slope of the coastal ranges. This void includes major parts of Washington, Oregon, California, Nevada, Utah, Colorado, Wyoming, Montana, Alberta, British Columbia, and apparently all of Idaho. We've never had a report of a martin being sighted in Idaho, although we've had a report from Missoula, Montana, and it seems unlikely that martins would reach Missoula without at least accidentally venturing through Idaho.

The northern limit of the western martin is somewhere along the coast of British Columbia or Alaska, but I'm not sure where. The most northern point from which we have had a reliable report of martins being seen was at Prince Rupert, British Columbia, near the southern tip of Alaska, but we have no nesting records farther north than the general area of Vancouver-Nanaimo-Victoria.

Martins in the coastal areas of British Columbia, Washington, Oregon and northern California nest in houses, including multiple-compartment houses, much more frequently than those in the southwest. They can be found around human homes, while those in the southwest rarely are.

Richard L. Todd, wildlife specialist of the Arizona Game and Fish Department, suggested both subspecies may exist in that state, with elevation being one of the determining factors.

"In Arizona," he wrote, "there are montane (Progne subis subis) and southern desert (P. s. hesperia) populations of purple martins. The desert race has been dependent upon stands of saguaro cacti and the mountain birds are found amongst somewhat open, snag-rich ponderosa pine forest. Population dynamics are something of a mystery because some nesting occurrences are somewhat irregular chronologically, and there are many seemingly suitable areas that do not seem to be occupied by breeding birds."

"Starlings," Todd added, "have not significantly invaded most of the Sonoran desert type as breeding birds, as yet, except near large towns. They are infrequent in our pine forests."

Stephen Russell, curator of birds at the University of Arizona, elaborated a bit more on martins there. "Southern Arizona martins are smaller (Progne subis hesperia) than eastern martins (P. s. subis). The race P. s. subis nests in northern Arizona and Washington and Oregon birds are also subis."

In 1982, biologist Virgil Scott of the Denver Wildlife Research Center added more on western martin occurrences.

Part of a large flock of martins are shown drinking and bathing at a pond in a gravel quarry on Silverbell Road near Tucson. This photo was taken in September, 1943, by Milam Cater.

The west does have purple martins, and many of them assemble in southern Arizona each year. This is just a small part of an enormous flock photographed in 1974 by Craig Wellman of the Tucson Daily Star and featured in an article by ornithologist Edward Chalif, then president of the Tucson Audubon Society.

"In addition to those nesting in saguaro cactus in southern Arizona, there are quite a few natural nesting purple martins along the Mogollon rim where ponderosa pine snags are present. The acorn woodpecker, which is a communal nesting bird, can provide in one snag several holes of a suitable size for martins. I have seen as many as 12 pairs of purple martins nesting in one snag near Cibecue on the Apache Indian reservation. Many of the ponderosa pine snags have been removed from the forests during timber cutting and fuel wood cutting and most forest dwelling martins have been forced into inaccessible and uncommercial tree stands.

"I have also seen nesting purple martins in southwestern New Mexico and western Colorado. The martins in Colorado apparently are not as communal in nesting as the Arizona birds, possibly because the acorn woodpecker is not present to provide holes. The Colorado birds, that I have seen, have been solitary nesters and were in aspen trees. They did, however, feed in small flocks during the breeding season."

THE TUCSON FLOCK

People of Tucson don't need proof that martins exist there. A huge assembly flock caused controversy there for several years. I can't say

Martins in the southwest nest almost exclusively in natural cavities. Two very important sources are ponderosa pine snags and saguaro cacti. This snag was photographed by Virgil Scott. This saguaro photo was among material accumulated by Milam Cater during a research project in the early 1940s. At least at that time, this was the largest saguaro in the world. It had 52 arms, weighed 10 tons, and had numerous woodpecker holes that were homes for several species of birds. If the man in this photo was six feet tall, the cactus was least 40 feet tall, and that's about the height of a four-story building.

whether the flock is still there, but it was just a few years ago when a lot of folks were unhappy about it.

The location was a clump of mulberry trees at East Grant Road and North Swan Avenue. Tens of thousands — a startling number for an area in which nesting martins are allegedly hard to find — gathered there each year from late summer until well into October.

Once undeveloped, the area had become a trailer park, and the big flock had made itself a real nuisance. The court's owner tried several things to discourage the birds, apparently without success. We haven't had a report on this flock for several years, so presume that it finally did shift to a new location.

1985 STATUS REPORT

The most thorough status report we've seen recently was published in 1985 by U.S. Fish and Wildlife's Portland office. That report said, in part:

"The western population of purple martins was once fairly common throughout its historical range in southern British Columbia, western Washington, western Oregon (including high elevations east of the Cascades) and California. Thriving colonies were formerly found in northwest towns and cities, e.g., Vancouver, BC; Seattle and Port Townsend, WA; and Klamath Falls, OR.

"However, since World War II, a drastic population decline has occurred, and colonies are reduced to a few pairs or have been extirpated. In Seattle only 32 martins were seen in the fall of 1980 compared to 12,500 in the fall of 1945. In California, a dramatic decrease has occurred in the southern coast range, where only 32 martins were found at three breeding locations in 1980. In Oregon, 300 breeding pairs were known in 1984 (nesting for the most part in pilings and nest boxes along the coast and the Columbia River, and in snags in the Coast Range and Cascade mountains), up from 168 pairs in 1977.

"Purple martins appear in low numbers on the Breeding Bird Survey, with 11-year averages (1968-78) of .032 birds per route in Oregon (having occurred on five routes over the 11 years), .025 birds per route in Washington (two routes), and .234 birds per route in California (27 routes). In Oregon, four of the five routes were along the southern coast, and one was near Wickiup Reservoir. In California, the species is now rare and local, and most of the routes getting martins are located along the coast and adjacent coast ranges north of Port Reyes. A lesser number of routes with martins were in the vicinity of the Diablo Mountains between Monterey and San Luis Obispo, and a small number of routes were located in interior California. Many of the California routes getting martins at higher elevations of the coast range seem to be in the vicinity of reservoirs."

THE LUND STUDY

Tom Lund of Oregon, who did a great amount of research on martins in the northwest during the 1970s, has been most emphatic in his efforts to eliminate the confusion that exists on western martins. In 1978 he wrote, ". . .most of the martins in the west are not of a different subspecies from those in the east. . .The only martins that belong to the 'western martin' subspecies are those nesting in saguaro cactus in Arizona and (in various types of nesting sites) in Baja California and adjacent parts of Sonora."

Lund is among those who believe martins can be attracted to multiple compartment houses with as much frequency as those in the east, and suggested the lack of opportunity is one of the main reasons they haven't been so attracted. In 1976 he wrote, ". . .this past season martins were packed as densely as possible into clusters of single unit boxes which are nailed up on snags in a manner that duplicates a single multiple-unit dwelling; there were many cases of three, four, and even five pairs of birds nesting right next to each other with no room to spare; and in one six-unit

During a survey of martins in the northwest in the mid-70s, Tom Lund found 200 pairs in 34 colonies — 68 of those pairs at Fern Ridge Reservoir, where this photo was taken. This was the site of much of his experimental work, as evidenced by the numerous single and multiple-compartment houses visible in lower center of this picture.

traditional style here there were four pairs of martins and one pair of tree swallows."

In 1978 he added, ". . .further evidence has been garnered indicating that martins in the west will indeed nest in multiple-compartment boxes just as they do in the east. The clusters of single-unit boxes at Fern Ridge Reservoir have been 80-100 percent full during the last three years, including one group of eight boxes, and the six-unit box made from an old drawer has consistently had four martin pairs and one pair of tree swallows; near Chiloquin, Oregon, a martin house on a pole many miles from water has seven or eight pairs in it this year, twice as many as last year."

At that time martins hadn't nested in large numbers in aluminum houses, but Lund theorized it may have had something to do with compartment size and a difference which does seem to exist between the eastern and western birds. Those western birds he studied produced larger broods on the average, and that may have accounted for a need for larger cavities.

Purple martins can be attracted to man-made housing in the west as these photos by Tom Lund in a western Oregon valley illustrated. Lund and others have called for more housing to build up the western population.

Dr. Stanley Richmond of Oregon maintained successful martin houses in the 1950s on the control house of this bridge over the Siuslaw River near Florence, Oregon. The birds were not bothered by the noise of the trains passing below them. Richmond authored in 1953 an extensive study of purple martins in the northwest.

These two successful sites are located near Waldport, Oregon, and among those researched by Tom Lund. House at left is owned by Ed and Barbara Thayer on Alsea Bay about a mile inland from the coast. Houses below belong to Dale Richardson and are along the Alsea River.

"Clutches average better than five," he wrote, "with six eggs occurring in a large percentage of the nests and seven eggs being not all rare.

"Almost all of the cavities in which I have located martin nests and have been able to examine closely have been a minimum of 12 inches deep and five to six inches in diameter; usually they are deeper and a number of them I have reached into the full length of my arm (34 inches) and still not hit bottom! Small cavities in snags and pilings (those which are 6x6x6) are never used, while larger ones nearby are used year after year."

That same year, however, Lund reported martins were starting to use some Trio TG-12s that had been erected at Fern Ridge as part of an experimental program. One of the houses had six nests. That house also had porch dividers to separate the compartments, and Lund said he felt that was a factor in getting that level of occupancy. While porch dividers proved unnecessary in early tests in the east, it well could be that martins in the west are more quarrelsome when nesting close together.

Finally, I want to comment on your chances of attracting martins in the west. During the past 20-plus years we have always made a point of not misleading inquirers about those chances. We may have overdone this to the point where a great many people think there is no chance at all. If so, this is unfortunate.

Mike Wege of the University of California at Davis discovered martins nesting in drainage holes in this expressway overpass at Sacramento. Each nest was built on a horizontal section about 12 inches up inside the hole. To make their lives a little easier, he erected two Trio aluminum houses nearby in a parking lot used by city buses.

Martins can be attracted in many communities, particularly those mentioned where the species is the same as the eastern martin. Tom Lund has worked very hard to encourage new martin projects. So have numerous others, chiefly in the northwest. One of the leaders in this new campaign is David R. Fouts of Portland.

And in 1985, the thrust of the U.S. Fish and Wildlife report was a new campaign to rebuild the martin population throughout its range. That report called for erection of many new nesting boxes, especially near existing colonies. Fish and Wildlife biologists feel the best chance may be in expanding these existing colonies into nuclei from which rapid growth can be achieved. Fouts is in an ideal location to do that.

If you do decide to attract martins, start looking for them March 1 in central California, mid-April in the Puget Sound area.

Chapter 9

The Purple Martin's Problems

Introduction

Every species of life has numerous other species and forces working to keep its numbers in check. Martins are no exceptions, even though their lives are easier than those of most species of wildlife.

Four major categories of "enemies" keep the martin population from growing as rapidly as some of us would like, and I have listed them in what I consider their overall order of importance: 1. Nest competitors; 2. Parasites; 3. Predators; 4. Weather.

Other things take occasional tolls — boys with guns, men with guns, poisons, disease — but these influences are minor compared to the "big four." In this chapter I'll discuss those four in the order mentioned above. In chapter 10 I'll tell you how to counter all these natural enemies and help your colony grow faster.

Subchapter A

Nest Competitors

Perhaps a dozen species of birds and mammals compete with purple martins for nesting cavities, but two small birds — starlings and house sparrows — dwarf all others in their importance. By themselves, these two imported species have caused a big decline in the populations of many native hole-nesting songbirds.

Their effect on the ecological balance of this continent has been so marked that some ornithologists have been calling for controls on starlings and sparrows for more than half a century. Some want eradication, but there's no agreement on how that could be achieved.

HOUSE SPARROWS

The house sparrow, often called the English sparrow, was first imported in 1850 when eight pairs were brought to New York state. Importation continued until 1883. Optimism was high, since bird enthusiasts thought they would control cankerworms and provide a cheerful addition to the landscape. Since that time, however, the house sparrow has spread over virtually the entire continent and shown an amazing ability to adapt to a variety of nesting sites and food, with apparently no effective natural enemy.

They are very prolific, each pair raising 3-4 broods per season. They remain in the neighborhood of their birth year around, and whatever ground they lose to other birds in housing battles during the summer is regained in winter, when they become firmly entrenched in any available cavities.

Although not actually a sparrow but a weaver finch, this is the only unpopular bird that carries the "sparrow" name. About 40 species — and many races — of the true sparrow family exist in North America, and among birders they are a popular group indeed.

Like all sparrows and finches, the house sparrow has a short beak, but its markings distinguish it from all other members of these families. Persons who plan some sort of action against house sparrows must be certain they have the correct bird. The male's markings include a black throat, white on the side of the head, and gray on top. His back, wings and tail are brown striped, and underside is gray. The female is a fairly uniform, soft brown with no distinguishing black or brown markings.

House sparrows consume many harmful insects, including termites, and a number of nuisance seeds, including crabgrass when available. In general, it is less an economic disaster than the starling, but the pressure it puts on native songbirds may be even greater.

Fortunately, the population is somewhat less than it was 50 years ago and overall seems to have stabilized. The problem has not mitigated, however, because the species has concentrated itself in villages and farm-steads. Their most aggressive nesting is near human activity, the very same places martins prefer.

Don Grussing, in his booklet, "How to Control House Sparrows" (Roseville Publishing House, Roseville, Minnesota), described a typical house sparrow tactic. In this case, a pair of sparrows had investigated a house only to find a pair of chickadees had already nested in it and just hatched eight eggs.

"The house sparrows, instead of moving on to find another house, stayed near the chickadee nest and repeatedly drove the parents away as the chickadees were trying to feed their young. It was pathetic to see the gentle chickadees land near the house, their tiny, pointed bills filled with squirming worms and tiny bugs, unable to get into the house to feed their young. As they would flit towards it, the sparrows would leave their perch at the top of the house or a nearby branch, and dive-bomb the smaller, less aggressive native birds. It was sad. The chickadees would hang around for a few minutes, then they would drop their prey and move along out back to the trees only to return in a few minutes with a fresh load of food. But their worried 'dee-dee-dee' complaints had little effect on the sparrows."

Quite often sparrows don't go to this much trouble. They simply start building right over an existing nest while the parent birds are away. They can build a nest in an amazingly short time. In only a day or two a pair of sparrows can stuff a compartment full and craft a nesting space well back inside it.

At Purple Martin Junction we have seen complete nests of martin eggs covered with new sparrow nests in 24 hours. Martins and other swallows seem particularly vulnerable to this because until brooding and feeding commences they usually go out every day on long feeding forays away from the nests.

EUROPEAN STARLINGS

The first starlings were imported into America in 1890 by a group that was determined to introduce every species mentioned by Shakespeare. Sixty were released in New York City's Central Park, and now the U.S., Canada and Mexico have millions of them from coast to coast.

They are very aggressive and usurp cavities of species ranging from wood ducks through woodpeckers to swallows, wrens and flycatchers. They often destroy eggs and young in the nests.

Starlings are often confused with martins, but are easily distinguished by their long bill, longer legs and more direct flight. In summer their bill is yellow and plumage dark, but in winter the bill turns dark and plumage becomes speckled. Photo at left is by Karl Maslowski; photo at right is by Joe Huber.

Starlings gather in huge flocks from late summer until spring. In cities they create both sanitation and noise problems. In the countryside they destroy grain crops valued in millions. They have caused staggering problems for livestock feeding operations. Some flocks are so large they consume tons of feed daily from livestock feeders.

Starlings are good fliers but spend a good deal of time on the ground. With their waddling gait, they patrol lawns and parks, using their long beaks to penetrate the matted material near the ground and grub under it for worms and insects. They rid lawns of some harmful insects, and include grasshoppers, white grubs and Japanese beetles in their diets. Like all birds, they are not all bad, but the damage they have done to our ecological structure outweighs their benefits.

Starlings are dark-colored, about the size of a martin, and at first glance are sometimes mistaken for martins. At second glance, however, the differences stand out. Starlings have long bills, short tails, and stand up on their legs when perched. Although they occasionally hover or soar in martin style, their normal flight is much more direct than the soaring, whimsical flight of the martin.

In spring and summer, the starling's bill is yellow and its body dull black. In winter, the bill turns dark and plumage becomes heavily speckled. The sexes look alike.

They throw together a nest of twigs and trash in a variety of places, but prefer dark cavities. They are commonly found nesting in walls of buildings, natural tree cavities, and in wooden martin houses that have been neglected.

In the '70s, Charles Brown illustrated the starling problem sharply in his study, "The Impact of Starlings on Purple Martin Populations in Unmanaged Colonies" (American Birds, May 1981). When management was discontinued in a group of test colonies, starlings took over.

By "management," Brown meant "general upkeep and maintenance of the martin colony, periodic sparrow and starling nest cleanout during the nesting season, cleaning and closing of martin houses when purple martins are gone, etc. In addition," he wrote, "where legal and feasible, some people manage their colonies by eliminating sparrows and starlings."

During this study he kept records on 18 colonies in Grayson County, Texas, during the years 1973-78. Ten colonies were managed during 1973-76 and then left unmanaged during 1977-78. As a "control," the remaining eight colonies were managed throughout. Here are the results:

Table 1. Average yearly number of purple martins and starlings at 10 colonies which were managed in 1973-76 and unmanaged in 1977-78.

Species	Pairs 1973-76	Pairs 1977-78
Purple Martin	108.3	42.0
Starling	2.1	25.5

Table 2. Average yearly number of purple martins and starlings at 8 colonies which were managed in 1973-78.

Species	Pairs 1973-76	Pairs 1977-78
Purple Martin	55.4	61.0
Starling	0.5	0.0

As you can see, the martin population dropped to less than half in just two seasons after management was discontinued, while the starling increased until they made up three-eighths of the colony's bird population.

Studies like this are tremendously important because they show so clearly the effect of these imported competitors.

TREE SWALLOWS

Tree swallows are small swallows with green backs and white breasts. They nest throughout the northern states and Canada and winter along the southern coasts. They are cavity-nesters, but nest in loosely scattered colonies, rarely more than one pair to a house. They are especially common on bluebird trails.

Unlike other swallows that rely entirely on flying food, these can pick

Great crested flycatcher,
by Steve Maslowski

Eastern bluebird,
by Alfred Francesconi

Some other popular species may occasionally show an interest in your martin house, although they usually prefer slightly different accommodations. The great crested flycatcher is a little woodland bird that usually includes a snakeskin in its nesting material. The eastern bluebird prefers single-cavity houses slightly more isolated from human activity. They flourish beside fields and open woodlots in houses at least 400 yards apart. And the house wren usually prefers a smaller cavity with smaller hole that excludes other species, but will raid martin houses, piercing eggs and throwing them out of the nest.

House wren,
by Alfred Francesconi

insects from vegetation, and even eat berries on occasion. Consequently, they are less vulnerable to weather, and often show up a week or two ahead of martins in the northern rage. That gives them an edge in househunting.

Although small and seemingly fragile, tree swallows are aggressive little scrappers, and one pair can keep martins from nesting in a house. They aren't one of the most common problems for martins, but we get a few reports almost every year from landlords who find tree swallows are all the problem they need. Some northern martin enthusiasts have even called for a reduction in their numbers, but with most bird enthusiasts they are popular.

OTHER COMPETITORS

Other cavity-nesters that occasionally compete with martins include great crested flycatchers (especially near forests), wrens, woodpeckers, and even bluebirds, but none of these is important. Squirrels, including flying squirrels, will nest in birdhouses, too, but not often. Squirrels seem to like a little less exposure than they get in a martin house.

Subchapter B

Parasites

Some might argue with my ranking this as the second most important threat to martins, claiming that actual losses of birds are not nearly as high as the nuisance factor suggests. The reasoning behind this is that parasites, by definition, depend on their hosts for their own survival, so it doesn't make sense they would go so far as to kill their hosts.

But I'm convinced losses are high. I've seen too many young birds driven from untreated houses by parasites on hot summer days — and too many young birds on the ground beneath unprotected houses and gourds. I've seen too many young birds underweight and sickly as they approach fledging time, and don't believe all these birds recover to become healthy, normal adults. And I've had too many reports of large and sudden losses of young birds — whole colonies wiped out — that have been attributed to parasites.

I'm convinced parasite control is almost as important as controlling starlings and sparrows.

Nest mites are the most common problem in our part of the midwest. We receive numerous complaints about blowflies from father east. Fleas are a problem in some regions. Blackflies have devastated some colonies in some of the northern and Great Plains regions. Numerous other parasites take a toll.

Tiny blood parasites, transmitted by mosquitoes, blackflies, and other blood-sucking insects, take a toll but the extent isn't well known because of the difficulty of positively identifying these conditions.

LeRoy Mather of Shakopee, Minnesota, shows why it is wise to check nests frequently, regardless of the parasiticide used in a nest. Until 1975 he regularly lost 50-75 percent of his young, and didn't know why.

In 1975 he learned the answer: maggots.

"I checked under the dry floor," he wrote, "and to my surprise, there must have been 100 maggots on the floor. These maggots were red inside from sucking blood from the young birds. . . They turned out to be the larvae of the grey cluster fly. These flies lay their eggs under the leaves of the cup of the nest. They are a fast growing maggot that suck blood out of the living birds. Allowed to do this, they will kill the young birds in a matter of days. As martins nest in the heat of the summer, the young birds, after dying, dry up in a few days. The maggots turn into flies and there is no evidence of what killed the young birds.

"This year, 1975, I kept checking the nests every week to see when the eggs hatched. In checking the nests after the martin eggs hatched, I again found fly larvae, which are very small when first hatched. (Full grown, they are about the size of a head on a wooden match and gray in color.) One by one, I changed all the nests with new nesting material — swamp grass works good. This was the first year, out of the last 10, that I had 100 percent survival rate."

Gordon Brainard of Hopkins, Michigan, had the same problem in 1975 and eventually lost 20 young birds. After discovering 13 dead, he cleaned out the nests, dusted with one percent rotenone, and replaced the nests with new ones of straw. A half-dozen or so more young ones that had been about ready to fly became frightened in the process and did fly and were lost. The remainder of his young — 55 or so — were raised successfully.

Many landlords are still reluctant to check on nests after nesting starts, fearful of scaring away parent birds, preferring to let nature take its course. I cannot agree with this.

Mrs. Henry R. Kaht of Antioch, Illinois, illustrates what can happen: "In the week or two that followed (hatching)," she wrote, "I simply let nature run the show and never peeked at the babies. Then one day to my horror I noted a baby bird floating on the water over which my martin house was situated. . .As I stood on the pier and lowered the house to check on the rest of the young I experienced a most ghastly sight. . .Here huddled in the nests were the young martin babies each with several maggots attached to their little bodies. Also was noted one dead fledgling. The remaining birds were next to dead."

With repeated dusting of the house, the Kahts eventually raised six young from the house that year.

In 1984, landlords throughout a wide area of Minnesota, Iowa and Nebraska were puzzled by the sudden death of young birds in their colonies. All losses seemed to occur during the last days of June and first few days of July. Many of these losses were discovered only when they noticed the old birds acting strangely, refusing to enter the houses to feed young, and then within a day or two abandoning the colonies. Most early reports indicated no obvious cause of death.

Several landlords had noted unusual swarms of what appeared to be gnats in their vicinities at about that time, but gave it no significance.

Some reports suggested a link, however, and a few did report an obvious — although not immediately obvious — cause of death. The young birds had been extensively bitten, with the heaviest concentrations on the tops of the head, neck and back. These bites were concealed by the feathers.

Subsequent investigations, including one by the Minnesota Department of Natural Resources, showed at least some of the losses — and probably most of them — were caused by blackflies, also commonly known as "buffalo gnats." These are vigorous little blood-sucking flies, about halfway between the sizes of a typical gnat and a typical housefly. They are most common in the north woods, and can reach plague numbers

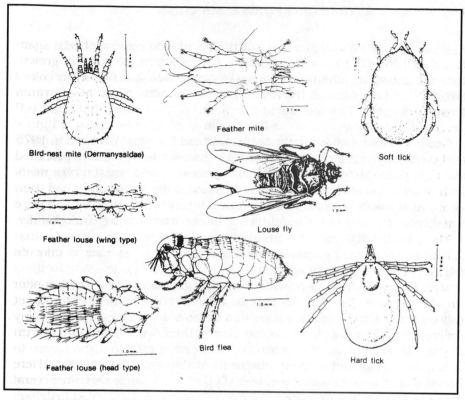

Feather mite

Bird-nest mite (Dermanyssidae)

Soft tick

Louse fly

Feather louse (wing type)

Bird flea

Hard tick

Feather louse (head type)

These eight, plus blowflies, are the parasites most often associated with purple martins. Bird-nest mites are the most commonly seen and can be found in huge numbers, appear like tiny specks crawling over compartment walls and the nesting material in it. Lice may actually be more common, but they never leave their host birds so won't be noticed unless a landlord captures a bird and inspects it carefully.

when water conditions are just right. They were just right in a wide area during those final days of June, 1984.

Fortunately, these situations are not common. And many of those 1984 losses could have been avoided if landlords had noticed those swarms and at that time lowered their houses and sprayed them with an insect repellent.

Finally, Alva Nye Jr., a widely respected naturalist of the Washington, D.C. area and a longtime martin enthusiast, suspected that parasites were a cause of some of those unexplained abandonments of whole colonies of young birds by their parents. As he told it:

"I speak from experience. My colony now (in 1975) is 25 years old. There are slightly over 300 breeding birds here in seven large houses. When the young are all on the wing, there are close to 1,000 birds around.

"Many years ago, before I took up sulfuring each apartment, I had a 28-

apartment house full of nesting martins. Suddenly, the old birds abandoned the house. All the young died. Investigation revealed the entire
house was literally alive with millions of almost invisible mites. The white
surfaces, upon close scrutiny, were gray with them. Some people think
they are lice, but they are mites.

"Each year, about two weeks before the martins are due back, I put a
round teaspoonful of sulfur in each apartment. I use commercial grade
sulfur because it is much less expensive than the kind you find in a drug
store. Without sulfur (or some similar pesticide) you are guaranteed to
have mite problems sooner or later, and lose baby martins."

If you think Nye's offhand reference to millions of mites is a wild
exaggeration, consider the following quote from Ewing (Auk XXVIII-
1911, pp 335-340), quoted from Michigan Bird Life:

"Careful experiment has shown that at least one species of chicken
mites, Dermanyssu gallinae, and probably the worst one, is perfectly at
home on the English sparrow, frequently swarms in its nests and after
multiplying freely on sparrows may be transferred again to chicks without
any loss of vitality. A single feather in a sparrow's nest was found to carry
72 living mites, and at least 250 similar feathers were found in this nest
giving a probable total of at least 18,000 in one nest."

Eighteen thousand mites in one nest! At that rate, a 12-compartment
house alone could contain around 200,000 mites. A single very large house
could have a million or more.

In 1983, when the Nature Society analyzed result of its study of
parasiticides, 38, 126 nest mites were counted in 64 nests, but half of them
— 19,330 mites — came from one untreated control nest alone. (In this
particular case five young did fledge successfully from that heavily infested nest, but I would not count on that happening every time.)

CAMIN AND MOSS

Some light on the most insidious effects of nest parasites was cast in the
1960s in an excellent study — **Nest Parasitism, Productivity and Clutch
Size in Purple Martins** — by entomologists W. Wayne Moss of the
University of California and Joseph H. Camin of the University of
Kansas.

The study was published in Science, Vol. 168, and is recommended
reading for the serious observer.

A series of carefully controlled tests were run on martin broods in a pair
of colonies established in 1964 in the Lawrence, Kansas, area. They kept
one colony free of parasites and allowed parasites to exist in the other.
They studied such things as the number of eggs per clutch in both
colonies, the rates of growth, survival rates, and sizes of young at fledging
time.

Their conclusions are important:

1. Parasite-free martins probably produce more eggs. "Modal brood size for parasitized and unparasitized martins was four, but there was a significant trend toward production of broods of five by mite-free birds, and of broods of three by parasitized parents."

2. Parasite-free martins produce larger young. "Martins in the absence of acarine nest parasites produced young heavier than parasitized young of the same brood size; in addition, unparasitized nestlings tended to reach a maximum weight equivalent to that of young in parasitized broods of one less member.

In short, the presence of parasites seems to reduce the productiveness of parent martins at every stage of the reproductive cycle.

The rat snake above had already eaten one baby wren when Steve Maslowski photographed it and would probably empty this nest before leaving. The snake below, killed by W. L. Pickhardt of Stillwater, Oklahoma, had eaten 11 martins, nine of which are shown in the picture. The photo at left by F. V. Williams of Gilbert, South Carolina, illustrates what most martin enthusiasts already know — poles are no problem for snakes. This one descending a post had just eaten several baby birds.

Predators

Range-wide, predators are no longer a serious threat to the semi-domesticated population of the purple martin, but to individual colonies they can be serious indeed. To landlords who have had entire colonies wiped out by owls, raccoons, or snakes, predators rank number one. In chapter 10 I'll explain how to prevent losses. In this chapter, however, I'll present a brief sketch of each type of predator, and I hope make a strong case for why prevention is necessary.

SNAKES

A five-foot snake can easily swallow a half-dozen martins or more in a single night's raid. Working in the disorienting conditions of darkness, a snake may manage to claim adults, young and eggs — a few of each — all in one night's work.

A majority of snake loss reports come from our southern correspondents, but terrain and environment actually has more to do with this than region. Houses near rivers, swamps and dense vegetation have a higher incidence of snake raids than those of more open and well manicured areas.

Principal culprits are king, corn, fox and rat snakes. Bull snakes, largest of the northern snakes (a black rat snake may grow as long but not as heavy), are rarely found around martin houses. Neither are eastern hognose snakes (puff adders), a snake that specializes in eating toads. Although rattlesnakes, copperheads and various water snakes are reputed to climb trees and eat birds, we rarely receive a report in which any of these types is involved.

Snakes and other predators are often suspected in cases of unexplained abandonment of a site. I suspect predator raids are, in fact, responsible for some of these abandonments. We've had numerous reports in which circumstantial evidence is convincing. A snake raids a house, eats the eggs or young, the parents leave the house and never come back, not that season or any other. . .

But neither is this automatic. We've had other reports — and these are a huge majority — of martins leaving a house after a big loss, but returning the next season.

I suspect martins are similar to some other species who abandon sites in which they have had poor nesting success. They do have some types of memory, and losing their broods in a particular location is a very useful thing to remember. Fortunately, most raids by snakes or any other predator do not take a large percentage of a colony's production, and do not seem to affect its existence very much.

OWLS

Four species of owls show up in our records as occasional killers of martins — great horned, screech, barn and barred. The first two are most common.

All four work almost always at night. Rarely is an owl satisfied with just one bird; sometimes they claim a surprising number in just one raid. Kenneth Vanhoy of Hallett, Oklahoma, lost 75-100 martins to owls during the 1976 season (although his big colony had a good season in spite of that).

In 1974, the Robert Hietts of Findlay, Ohio, watched a great horned owl visit their colony every half hour after midnight, taking six or eight birds a night during his raids. They believe this owl was the cause of unex-

This deadly duo accounts for most night losses of martins to predatory birds. The 20-inch great horned owl (photo by Alfred Francesconi) and the 8-inch screech owl (photo by Steve Maslowski) both range over almost all of the martin's range. Range-wide, they aren't much of a problem, but to occasional individual colonies either one can be a big problem. Several other owl species have also been reported taking martins in night raids, but these seem to be rather rare.

The American kestrel is a pretty little falcon that sometimes kills small birds, but not martins. Cases of kestrels killing martins are extremely unusual.

plained losses they had suffered for several years. Despite the losses, their colony survived and these birds gave no hint of abandonment.

Steven Kroenke lost approximately 50 birds to a Florida barred owl in one season, but that colony survived.

John and Dorothy Skelton's colony at Brightwood, Virginia, was invaded by a horned owl in 1985 and they saw their production of young drop by more than 100 over that of the previous year. But that colony survived even a loss like that.

Unlike snakes, which consume their prey on the spot and usually leave little or no evidence, owls tend to carry their prey to a particular spot (this is by no means universal) where it is consumed. In Vanhoy's case that was a nearby basketball goal. He wrote that on three occasions he found wing feathers of a large number of birds under that goal.

While feeding, owls sometimes drop less attractive parts, and occasionally eject pellets of undigestible parts. A variety of materials may be found under a spot used by an owl for eating.

HAWKS

Hawks are not much of a problem for martins because most of them don't fly well enough to catch a martin. The notable exceptions to this are three small woodland hawks — Cooper's, sharp-shinned and goshawk. These, too, are usually unable to capture a martin in open flight, but some are able to surprise martins during leisure flight around the colonies.

Donald L. Sheldon of South St. Paul, Minnesota, was puzzled by a gradual loss of birds at his colony near Park Rapids. It had dropped from 35 adults to 25 adults when he finally discovered the culprit. He first found a sharp-shinned hawk on the ground with a martin in its talons, but wasn't certain how it had captured the bird. He thought it unlikely the hawk could have caught it on the wing, but a few days later he saw another hawk knock a martin into the lake and realized "the hawk was taking the birds on the wing as they glided in the wind." But he also noted that year that "the martins were wising up and were flying in more evasive patterns after the hawk began taking them."

We don't know whether Sheldon's martins adjusted to the sharp-shin threat, but Steven Kroenke's colony had an obviously more serious threat from a Cooper's hawk in 1980. It was an eye-opening experience.

"Late one afternoon in mid-February," he wrote, "I was observing my martins as they flew in to roost. It was nearly dark, and most of the martins had settled down, except for a few stragglers, which were flying from one gourd to another, trying to find a place to sleep.

"Suddenly, a male martin screamed the danger call and streaked into the darkness, and right behind him was a large, brown bird. A hawk!. . .For a minute or so a small group of martins circled warily overhead; then in a flash all came thundering down and disappeared in the gourds and houses. The hawk did not return that evening. . .

"The next evening the hawk returned and made a spectacular attack on my colony, plummeting through the air, a feathered bullet, jerking from side to side as it attempted to catch a martin. The martins went berserk, scattering in all directions and eventually forming a unified flock that circled overhead. The hawk quickly disappeared into a black gum swamp about 50 yards from my colony.

"The evening attacks continued throughout the remainder of February and into the first week of March. . .I hadn't seen the hawk actually catch a martin; however, it was apparently successful — eight established male martins disappeared during those weeks. . ."

Later he did see the Cooper's take an adult martin, and still later in the season saw it make easy pickings of fledglings coming home to roost in the evening. Sometimes he was able to scare the hawk away from the area by standing among the houses and waving his arms.

As a result of his experience, Kroenke reached these tentative conclusions about Cooper's hawks:

1. Large, active colonies near heavy forest and swamps may attract them. 2. "His" hawk usually attacked in late evening and remained unnoticed until it was not more than 100 feet from the colony. 3. Although martins are superior in open flight, they cannot out-accelerate this hawk and can escape only by dodging it. 4. Martins readily attack a Cooper's if they see it ahead of time, but these attacks did not deter his hawk at all. 5. A Cooper's can take a heavy toll of young martins inexperienced in flying.

Kroenke said his hawk that season took at least nine established adults and caught some stragglers and young birds as well.

One other member of this family deserves at least a mention. American kestrels, more commonly known as sparrow hawks, are colorful little falcons that nest in cavities and occasionally capture small birds. We've had a few reports of them capturing young martins, but it's very uncommon.

A most intriguing such report came in 1982 from Mildred B. Read of Blairstown, New Jersey. She had kestrels nesting in a flicker house for three years. The first two of those years she had a pair of tree swallows in a martin house; the third year a pair of martins.

But the result each year was the same. A kestrel perched on the house just as the parent swallow did when it brought food. When a young bird appeared to be fed — it was promptly eaten. After the third season the flicker house was closed, and the kestrel forced to move on.

For the most part, however, kestrels prefer feeding over open terrain. They hunt by hovering or perching on wires while searching the ground for prey. Most of that prey consists of mice, voles and other tiny rodents; grasshoppers and other large insects; and a variety of other small life, including some slow-moving birds.

Finally, loggerhead shrikes may be capable of killing martins, but we do not receive reports of this happening. This little gray predator bird with distinctive black eye mask, usually prefers smaller game.

NEST-ROBBERS

Several species of songbird do not prey on adult martins, but occasionally raid nests. Best-known are blue jays, starlings and grackles. House sparrows and house wrens also ruin nests by either cracking eggs or rolling them out of the houses. Sparrow and wren activities, as well as some of that of starlings, are probably motivated by nest site competition rather than hunger.

None of these species is a threat to the population of purple martins or any other species. A certain amount of this type of depredation is a normal part of nature.

RACCOONS

Raccoons are woodland creatures that often live even within the boundaries of cities. They are clever, adaptable mammals able to climb well, and equipped with hands that can solve simple puzzles such as door latches and gate pins. They can even climb steel mounting posts less than two inches in diameter.

They are night feeders, and sometimes two or three may be found feeding together. A few 'coons can take a toll.

Fortunately, raccoons are so versatile in their diet they need not concentrate on one thing. If you've ever watched a 'coon feeding by a stream, carefully washing anything it picks up (even bread pieces which repeatedly disintegrate in its hand), you would think they are extremely "ticky" eaters. Apparently not so.

They consume a very wide variety of fruit, grains, leaves, tender shoots, berries, insects, crustaceans, reptiles, small mammals, birds and eggs. They are obviously voracious eaters; a few raccoons can strip the kernels from ears of an entire garden corn crop in a single night — or claim the young from an entire martin house.

Raccoons, like this one photographed by Alfred Francesconi, have been known to climb steel poles, and they can be very damaging to a martin colony if they can reach it. Opossums can, too, but I haven't known of a case where one of these has actually climbed a steel pole. This family of 'possums was photographed by the late Elmer Shoemaker of Waverly, Ohio.

OPOSSUMS

'Possums are somewhat similar to 'coons in their night feeding habits, climbing ability, and flexible diet. Raids on martin houses are not very common, however, and we have very little information in our files about these animals as problems.

CATS

Ordinary cats would like to be a bigger problem than they are. Even a well fed cat sometimes finds it hard to resist the urge to pounce on a bird.

Many noted bird-lovers have been devoted cat-haters, and have dedicated a lot of thought to finding ways to protect songbirds from them at feeders and nesting sites.

That feeling isn't unanimous. Les Line, longtime editor of Audubon magazine, for example, thinks cats are overrated as bird-killers. He said they are too well fed to be serious threats to songbirds.

Ornithologist William George agrees, and his opinions came as a result of carefully monitoring the habits of several cats for four years.

Perhaps domestic cats, being well fed and more limited in their freedoms, are not a serious threat, but countless feral, or semi-domesticated cats roam the countryside, and I agree with those who feel they take a big toll of birdlife.

Very few of these lost birds are martins, however, because cats cannot reach most martin houses; martins rarely land on the ground; and usually when they "strafe" an intruding cat they are careful not to dive too close (not always). These factors are fortunate, because cats are very effective predators. They are quick, agile, accurate, and have the surprising ability to jump straight up six feet or more. And they see well at night.

SQUIRRELS

When a martin house is not properly located, squirrels can figure as both potential nest competitors and nest robbers. They occasionally nest in wooden houses, and can quickly enlarge a wooden entrance hole to suit their tastes.

They have been known to kill young martins in houses they have been able to reach. Squirrels normally depend on a diet of nuts and other vegetable matter, so I'm not sure how often they would kill nestlings even if given the opportunity.

I suspect they normally would ignore nestlings unless they wanted to take over a compartment for their own use. While they rarely have access to martin nests, they do have frequent access to nests of robins, grackles, orioles, and other tree-nesters, and obviously are not a threat to those species.

The above is not an all-inclusive list of wildlife species that can cause problems in a martin house, but covers most of those you are apt to be concerned with. Nature is full of surprises and it is best to regard with some suspicion any type of wildlife that develops a sudden interest in your martin house.

Weather

While weather sometimes causes spectacular losses, I believe most of the best publicized weather problems have little or no effect on the general population picture. In this section, I'll discuss two types of problems.

The first, early spring cold snaps, sometimes kill off early arrivals but these, we think, are never critical to the population. One theory, believe it or not, holds they may actually benefit the population by killing off some domineering older birds and making it easier for young birds to move into established colonies.

The second, late spring or early summer periods of sustained cold winds and rain, can cause serious losses in an area, claiming eggs and nestlings as well as some parent birds. These are the problems that can require three years or more to recover from. They nearly always are local or regional in nature, and I suspect even these have little effect on the overall population.

EARLY SPRING PROBLEMS

Almost every year the Nature Society News learns of some areas in which weather is causing concern. Invariably, the northern states will experience at least one or two periods of cold lasting for a couple of days or so. Temperatures will fall into the 40s — even the 30s — insects will stop flying, and martins will huddle in their houses.

If the condition lasts more than two days, many martins pack themselves into single compartments — as many as 29 have been reported in a single compartment and 12-15 is common. But seldom do these cold snaps endure past the four days necessary to cause widespread mortality.

Sometimes they do. A severe case occurred in 1982, when prolonged cold hit many northern areas, including Purple Martin Junction. Of our first 15 birds that showed up that year, 14 died. Here's how the News reported that case:

"Scouts showed up in the north pretty much on schedule — March 20 in Griggsville is typical — and a few permanent arrivals showed up on March 31, April 1 and 2 — 15 birds in all.

"But the weather was never really great, and by April 6 it was awful. . .Wednesday, April 7, was worse. That morning, all 15 of our birds were found packed in one compartment. When the house was lowered, unaware it was full of birds, they flushed. All but one. It was dead.

"Thursday was still worse. Again the birds were back in that compartment. They flushed again as we approached. They were active and seemed healthy. . .

". . .we installed a 200-watt light bulb in a compartment of an adjoining house, closed that compartment, and allowed it to heat the other rooms of the house. . .curious to know whether they would pass up the original house in favor of a warmer one a few feet away. They used neither.

"Friday we found three dead on the ground, two others dead in compartments. Only two live birds were still in evidence. But the heavy snow was melting away rapidly that day, and we had some hope.

"Sunday afternoon, April 11, at 3 o'clock, one old male martin sat hunched on house number 1 at the far north end of the Society grounds. He was the only survivor. The temperature was in the 50s, the sun was shining, but the Junction was silent except for the occasional twitter of a sparrow or two.

"By 4:30, however, another martin was seen at the grounds, and sometime between then and 8 a.m. the next morning four more martins had checked in. They were all active, but that one survivor was still sitting alone, rarely moving. Gradually that one, too, began to show some new enthusiasm. Things were looking up.

"Monday, April 12, we began treating the houses for our (parasite) testing program, and later that week. . .large numbers of newcomers flocked in. We had a couple days of sunny weather and the air over the Junction came alive. It was beautiful."

Losses were scattered over quite a wide area that year, so we later

Here are a couple of pictures that show that weather problems can happen almost anywhere. The left photo was made by George Esler near Green Bay, Wisconsin, but the other was taken at the J. H. Pepper residence at Yazoo City, Mississippi (in late March, 1968). Both colonies survived.

surveyed members on the cold snap of early April, 1982, accumulated a substantial amount of information, and Jamie Hill organized and analyzed that information. Ultimately, he published the results of that study, and they're worth mentioning because that storm proved to be a record-setter.

The main conclusion of Hill's report was that this nine-day period of April 3-11, 1982 — commonly referred to as the "Easter storm" — spanned 25 states and Ontario and caused the most widespread mortality among a single species of wildlife that has been recorded. (Not necessarily the largest numbers, but the most geographically widespread.)

These losses may actually have helped the population by killing off older dominant birds. Certainly nothing in the News contradicted that. Letter writers reported some big losses that year, but at the end of that season most of them reported having seasons as good as usual, and some were better.

Those early losses seem to have affected the population not at all.

LATE STORMS

Hurricane Agnes is the classic example of a late sustained storm that kills off much of a season's production of young martins, and slows growth in an area. This happened in June, 1972, as the tail end of Agnes swept over the states of Pennsylvania, Maryland, the Virginias, Ohio, and

Bud's Citrus Center at Inverness, Florida, had one of the best martin set-ups around until Hurricane Gladys ripped through that community in 1968. But the five modern aluminum martin houses survived intact even though the post on which three of them were mounted was uprooted from the ground.

some adjoining areas.

Temperatures dropped into the 40s, and cold, drenching rains swept the area for up to four days.

Norman Conner of Delaware, Ohio, lost 83 young, 10 adults, and four nests of eggs. One nest of three survived. Oliver Watson of Canton, Ohio, lost 93 young and 15 adult females. Mrs. Robert Hiett of Findlay, Ohio, lost 29 young plus some eggs. J. O. Albert of Forest, Ohio, lost half his young from a colony of 50 pairs.

Bruce Blystone of Greensburg, Pennsylvania, reported on five colonies that lost all their young, and another that lost 75 young and some older birds. Two of those wiped out colonies were in the famous martin houses in Ligonier and Somerset.

P. J. Campbell of East Brady, Pennsylvania, lost more than 100 young birds. So did Ethel and Clyde Hoover of Circleville, Ohio. Carroll Arnold of Gibralter, Pennsylvania, reported all 21 young dead in his house. Allen Scranton of Wellsboro, Pennsylvania, lost 20 of 29 adults, and all of their young.

Charlie Elliott of Hampton, Virginia, lost his birds and reported all of his friends in Hampton and Norfolk lost from one-half to all of theirs. Edith Swadley of Harrisville, West Virginia, lost 32 young and some adults. John W. Skelton of Brightwood, Virginia, lost 80 young and one adult.

Mike Reed of Barboursville, West Virginia, reported on five colonies in a one-block area that lost a total of 64 young, 28 eggs and several adults. James Sponseller of Lakeville, Ohio, had 25 active nests and lost all of them.

And so it went. Agnes took the largest single toll we have had reported in the two decades we have been active in this field.

Kathy Klimkiewicz, whose research work is centered in Maryland and Virginia, all within the devastated area, said recovery there required three seasons. Some colonies never did recover. They were abandoned after the loss and not reoccupied the following spring.

By and large, the effects of Agnes passed, just as others have, but not for some landlords. Today, almost 15 years later, we still receive occasional letters from persons who lost their colonies that year and never regained martins.

Although storms are credited with a lasting decline of martins in New England, I doubt that storms alone could be responsible for long-term decline. If the New England population did not, in fact, recover, I suspect other factors combined with weather to inhibit that recovery — starlings, sparrows, urbanization, clean forestry and farming, and other modern factors.

While 1972 was tough in the Middle Atlantic region, 1974 was more of a problem for Canada. In June, Lorne Scott reported:

"The first purple martin arrived in Saskatchewan on schedule this

On July 4, 1969, Robert Reiniche of Horton, Michigan, was looking directly at this martin house from a distance of about 100 feet when lightning struck it and "pieces just seemed to disappear. . .smoke rose from the remains despite the downpour. . ." Within minutes, however, nearly 200 martins from the area gathered around the house with a noisy concern that lasted for three hours. The surviving parents went to work feeding the surviving babies, even feeding some through a broken floor and others by crawling down a central air shaft to reach them. Some died in the house, some charred babies were found at the base of the shaft, but many others survived.

spring in late April. By the middle of May landlords had their usual number of tenants. . .

"On May 18 a five-day rain began and brisk easterly winds kept the temperatures in the 30-45 degree range. . .The first records of martins suffering. . .were received by the Saskatchewan Museum of Natural History on May 22. Two people found martins lying on the ground beneath their colonies, too weak to fly. . .

Relief didn't come until May 24 when the sun shone and the mercury climbed to 65. Although Scott's associates rescued 58 birds and saved 56 of them during that period, losses were widespread. He summarized:

"The exact percentage of martins which did perish is impossible to determine. It would be safe to say that nearly every colony lost some birds. The area affected was at least 150 miles wide and 200 miles long, extending from Moose Jaw, Saskatchewan to Reston, Manitoba. It seems that few colonies were completely wiped out, but it will take at least two or three good years for many to fully recover."

I don't know how long it did take, but as I've mentioned, many colonies that are hit that early recover very quickly.

Farther east that year, Leo Roos of Ottawa lost 25 mature birds at his colony at a service station, but all 14 pairs at his sister's colony in the same vicinity survived. His sister's entire colony was absent during that critical period, and reappeared safe and sound afterward. Roos was convinced they had temporarily flown south far enough to avoid the severest weather. Some pretty heavy observers have found the idea credible.

"Occasionally martins do retreat south again," wrote Allen and Nice. "In the Chicago region on March 26, 1950, there was a strong east-southeast wind with a mean temperature 13 degrees F. above normal, on March 27 a strong southwest wind, mean temperature 14 degrees above normal; on the 27th a remarkable number of birds of many species had arrived. On the 28th the wind had changed to west-southwest, the temperature was 4 degrees below normal. About 8 on the morning of the 27th James Decker saw a number of birds, several martins among them, flying south, 10 to 14 hours before the advent of the cold front."

The Allen-Nice study also reported:

"Williams (1950: 58) writes: 'In late afternoon on March 22, 1947 I saw several large flocks of ring-billed gulls. . .many bank swallows. . .a few chimney swifts. . .and purple martins. . .migrating **southeastward** into a brisk and warm southeast wind. The first warm wave of the spring had surged up from the south a day or two previously, had occupied all the Gulf states, and had ascended the plains states as far as northern Nebraska. At the same time, however, a cold front was just entering the northwest corner of the United States. But this cold front did not reach Houston till about 40 hours after I had seen the birds migrating southeast."

But back to that 1974 season in Canada for one more example. The most robust of the extreme northeastern colonies belonged to Mr. and Mrs. Phil Downey at Pointe du Chene, on the eastern coast of New Brunswick. That year they had 37 pairs nest successfully and fledge 218 young, despite losing around 50 birds in May.

"The scouts that year arrived May 9 and four days later we had a cloud of about 50 birds that arrived on a south gale with sunshine and temperature at 60 degrees. . .On May 14 the chorus in the morning was very welcome, temperature was up to 70 degrees and we thought we had our birds for the summer.

"But during the night we had a thunderstorm and the temperature went below freezing again and there was even a little snow at times. The martins flew valiantly for about 10 days, and then started to look very sick and sad indeed. We don't know how they existed, cold and hungry and not a mosquito or fly in sight.

"On May 27 they started to drop. . .By May 30 there wasn't a martin alive in the community. . .But in spite of this disaster, other martins began to show up on June 1 and more arrived every few days throughout June and July. The last pair, a young couple, built a nest the last week in July."

J. P. Perron of St. Jean, who has one of the older and more flourishing colonies in Quebec, observed that males seemed more susceptible than females during that harsh spring. "In early May," he wrote, "large numbers of adults, more males than females, started dying of intestinal flu due to malnutrition caused by scarcity of insects in flight. . .The birds suffering. . .would die in approximately two hours after being observed. Artificial feeding did not help. I lost over 20 percent of my old birds. . .The loss in general through the region varied from 15 to 30 percent. . ."

Finally, lest you think this is just a northern problem, consider Kay McCracken's 1966 account in the Corpus Christi, Texas, Caller-Times:

"That monsoon we had the first week of May was a boon to some, a bane to others. Among bird people, too. Those who were just out looking — and probably more were out looking this time than ever before — saw, immediately following the downpour, one of the truly fabulous migrations of all times. All sorts of birds, including such rarities as western tanagers at Flour Bluff and bobolinks at Rockport, were seen.

"But there was another side to the coin. Those who had purple martins just bringing off young, sadly and helplessly watched their colonies weaken and die during the unseasonable rains. Dead and dying birds were picked up soaked, chilled and starving. None could be saved.

"Disasters occurred all over the area," she wrote, and then, after citing numerous examples, concluded, "The rain was just too abundant. Insects were plentiful, mosquitoes abundant — as everybody knows. One good hour of flying weather each day might have saved them.

Miscellaneous Problems

Numerous incidental factors cause occasional martin deaths. Losses to cars, guns and freaks of nature such as lightning can be disheartening, but not broadly significant. In chapter 10, I will mention some things that may be useful in preventing these problems, but for this section, suffice it to say they are not serious threats to the population.

Two other factors may be. These include pesticides and diseases.

Pesticides are being treated in this book as a minor problem, but may not be. Effects can be subtle and difficult to measure. I have downgraded this subject in this book simply because we receive fewer reports these days of large-scale die-offs that can't have other causes. I hope our impression is correct that pesticide residues are not the factor they were in the 1960s, when many species high in the food chain were declining.

I recognize that many people may simply have given up trying to identify mysterious losses, and no longer report them. I also hasten to point out that we are still very concerned about the use of chemicals in the environment. We're still conservative on this subject, recognizing that many chemicals have valuable uses, but that the thousands in use offer great potentials for danger, too. I'll talk a bit more about proper uses in chapter 10.

In the 1960s, scientists learned that eagles, ospreys and falcons were declining because thin-shelled eggs were ruining their reproductive success. Further study showed DDT was the cause, and this concentration of DDT was occurring because these raptors were high in "food chains." The animals eaten by these raptors carried high concentrations because they too were predators. They eat animals that eat smaller animals that eat smaller animals that eat smaller animals, and so on. At each step in that chain, pesticide residues become more concentrated.

Following removal of DDT and certain other pesticides from the U.S. market, the big raptors began to recover. Today, in the mid-80s, their populations are slowly increasing and even peregrine falcons have been successfully reintroduced in a few of their former habitats.

TWO EFFECTS

Poisons represent two types of possible dangers. The first includes obvious cause and effect. Martins suddenly die off because they have eaten poisoned insects, flown through poison spray, drank from ponds with poison spray floating on their surface, had their house directly sprayed, or some other such circumstance. Over the years we've had reports that fall in this category:

"In perfectly fine weather," a typical report reads, "the birds just start dying. Several of the birds in my colony were dead in their compartments and several more fell to the ground and died." And, "These birds experienced tremors before dying and they must be poisoned." Or, "We lost about half our colony last year after the city sprayed for Dutch elm disease; they didn't spray this year and we haven't lost a single bird."

The late Dr. T. E. Musselman, who was among the first to be deeply concerned about the growing use of pesticides, recounted this experience:

"Several years ago, I planned to band the young wrens in 18 boxes along the Hillcrest summer home area at the Sequanota Club, at Charlevoix, Michigan. A traveling agent of a spraying concern convinced the board of directors at the club grounds that the pine trees were infested with rust and a virus disease and should be sprayed. I warned them against the intrusion but the spraying occurred, and the wind carried the poisonous mist from pines to the deciduous trees and bushes. No doubt hundreds of small birds were affected, as it was the height of the nesting season.

"Thousands of worms and caterpillars hung from the trees with threads, and after wriggling in their death agonies, were picked up by the busy wren parents and fed to their young. Before the spraying there were about 100 young wrens about large enough to warrant banding and, of course, their flight was but a few additional days away. Unfortunately, the diet of poisoned bugs reduced their numbers until I could find but three babies which were alive and these were in the last box, the unit farthest away from the spraying activities."

In most cases, bird lovers don't have their dead birds analyzed. It's difficult to find a source, but it's worth a try. If you have a significant number of birds that die at the same time and there is no apparent cause, here are some possible courses of action:

1. Ask your veterinarian. Sometimes he can immediately identify the cause, especially if it is disease-related. If he can't identify it, he may be able to suggest a laboratory that will analyze it. Don't be surprised, however, if he has none to suggest. Chemical analysis is an expensive project, and labs willing to undertake gratis projects are not common.

2. Ask the local agent for your state department of conservation or natural resources. Specify your area's nongame biologist, if there is one.

3. Call the ornithology or natural history department of your nearest university. You might get lucky and find one with a special interest in this subject, and access to a laboratory.

4. Check with your local federal game agent. The U.S. Fish and Wildlife Service may be able to steer you to a source.

5. Don't give up. Your particular state may have other agencies with an interest.

Unfortunately, the evidence against certain chemicals as killers of birds is almost always more circumstantial than positive.

The case of Walter McKinley of Bertrand, Missouri, was reported in the Charleston, Missouri, Enterprise-Courier. McKinley had built up his colony to around 80 mature birds and in less than a week lost all but 15 or 20 of them. The Enterprise-Courier reported that ". . .when his birds started dying. . .(he) felt he was losing some old friends. 'In one three-day period I lost 65 of the mature birds,' Mr. McKinley said, 'and 47 little ones that had not started to fly.' Other varieties of birds were also found dead, Mr. McKinley said.

"The Bertrand resident is not eager to start any fights, but he blames crop spraying for the bird deaths. 'All I know is that a man sprayed a nearby field and not an hour later the birds started falling out of the houses,' he said.

"Conservation agent Art Province is not sure what is killing the birds. He says, however, that several people maintaining the special martin houses report the loss of their flocks. Many are found dead, while others have merely stopped appearing at the boxes, in some instances leaving baby birds without a source of food."

Circumstantial evidence? Unfortunately, yes. Other things could have caused these deaths.

Donald J. Siems of Bricktown, New Jersey, reported his mature martins abandoned his houses the evening after a spray plane made repeated, very low passes over his neighborhood during the day. When he investigated the 12 baby martins in the houses were dead. He inquired and found the chemical used was malathion, which is supposed to be safe for birds.

More circumstantial evidence. We have had quite a few of these reports over the years, but they don't prove anything except that someone should get a few of these group deaths analyzed and find out what caused them. If no chemicals show up as culprit, then we could presume diseases or parasites are causes. If some chemicals do show up, this is information the public should have. It would give added weight to the protests of citizens who do not want their yards sprayed.

During the 1984 blackfly plague in the Minnesota-Iowa area, incidentally, the Minnesota Department of Natural Resources got involved and did have some of the birds analyzed. These tests proved conclusively that poisons were not involved.

DISEASES

Bird diseases are too broad a subject to cover in this book, but they do account for many losses. Pneumonia and intestinal infections seem to be the major killers. Just as with humans or any other animals, weather and general physical conditions, and genetic weaknesses make martins more or less susceptible to diseases. Many birds killed by cold weather actually die of pneumonia or other diseases.

Martins are also susceptible to blood parasites, although the extent of this isn't clearly known.

Genetic weaknesses account for some losses. Sometimes apparent injuries prove to be physical abnormalities present since birth. These birds rarely survive to maturity and, if they did would not be equipped to survive independently. Nature still operates on a principle known as "survival of the fittest" or at least "non-survival of the unfittest."

It is probably best that abnormal birds die quickly. There may even be such a thing as mercy killings, although I doubt this would involve the same emotions we associate with that. There almost certainly is a process of rejection that occurs in some nests with deformed young.

In 1975, Robert A. Wolcott of North Platte, Nebraska, reported, "No cripple this year, but in previous years several deformed half-grown young pushed out of the nest by parents almost every year."

If you have a serious interest in bird diseases, books are available. The Kalamazoo, Michigan, Nature Center briefly discusses nearly a dozen of the common ones in its very useful **Wild Animal Care and Rehabilitation Manual**. This book, authored by Patricia Adams and Vicki Johnson, is available from the Nature Center, 7000 N. Westnedge Ave, Kalamazoo, MI 49007.

Not the most up-to-date, but an interesting book to start with is **Stroud's Digest of the Diseases of Birds**. It's a useful book made more interesting by the fact that its author was Robert Stroud, "the birdman of Alcatraz."

Stroud, you may recall, spent 54 years in solitary confinement, more than any other person we know about in history. The movie about his life stressed his friendship with the birds so much that many viewers may not have realized the scope of what he accomplished. In a sense, he was not totally solitary, because somehow, presumably through the mail, he communicated a great deal with other authorities and birders.

Stroud's Digest, originally published in 1943, is a hardbound book of nearly 500 pages, with diseases and other subjects discussed in alphabetical order. It isn't a very good reference to use for quick analysis, because it does not offer a systematic approach.

But it includes a ton of information, much of which is probably still accurate, and an interesting introduction to this subject.

Stroud obviously was more than a lonely man who needed the companionship of the birds. He was a very intelligent man who made a serious and valuable contribution to the science of healing birds. For the benefit of those who want to obtain a copy, the present edition was published by T.F.H. Publications, Neptune, New Jersey.

Chapter 10

Attracting Purple Martins in the 20th Century

MAXIMIZE YOUR CHANCES

In earlier times, almost any kind of martin house could be erected with reasonable expectation of success. Today, however, you need to follow some simple management practices to have that same chance.

Conditions have changed during the past century. Disappearing nest cavities and competition from starlings and sparrows have altered the picture drastically.

Our past 20 years of experience has shown us certain practices are now important, and they fall into three categories: (1) proper house design; (2) proper location; and (3) control of nesting problems. First, however, I want to talk about something that has not been so widely discussed: your attitudes and expectations.

These may influence your success; they definitely will determine your satisfaction.

First, try to look at your yard as a martin would. View the terrain, buildings, trees, animals — and humans — that make up the environment you are asking martins to inhabit. This can be an intriguing, but practical, little mental exercise, and is almost certain to increase your chances.

Find the spot in your yard that would seem to you — if you were a martin — to offer good security from predators, good views of open space for random flight around the house, and for seeing random insect food in the neighborhood. And you probably should be sure the spot has a view — from a safe distance of course — of human traffic around the home. I believe martin houses exposed to human homes have more appeal than ones shielded from view by other buildings or trees.

Second, develop reasonable expectations. You may not attract martins the first year, or the second, or even the third — you may eventually have to change the location of your house. Realize your start may be slow, but the first pair will make it worthwhile, and once a colony is started, success is almost always continual year after year.

Develop reasonable expectations about insect control, too. You can expect to see fewer of all kinds of flying insect pests around your home once martins are established, but do not expect 100 percent control of any species. Nature doesn't work in 100-percent terms.

After you have a few pairs in residence, I am sure you will be pleased with their effect on your yard.

What are your real chances? If you follow good housing, location and management practices, they should be very good.

A survey in the summer of 1983 showed that 92 percent of the people who read the Nature Society News (the "purple martin paper") have martin housing available in their yards, and of these, two-thirds do have martins. Of the remaining one-third, fully half have had housing up only 1-3 years, not long enough to justify being discouraged.

This meant only one-sixth of the readership was having real problems. Of these, a small percentage had had martins previously but lost them for unexplained reasons. And a certain percentage inevitably have their houses in the wrong location or are failing for some other correctable reason.

I believe that attitude itself — one of the most intangible of factors — can be one of the most important. Martins certainly relate to humans in some provable ways, and maybe some others as well. Let me cite an obvious example of martins developing a feeling of security around certain individuals.

Tom Coulson's father, George, has a colony at the edge of Versailles, Illinois. A couple of years ago, Tom decided to take some pictures at this colony. He sat quietly in a chair only 15 feet from one of the poles, without any type of concealment, confident the birds would soon return to their house and the young birds in it.

After 20 minutes without any sign of activity around the house, the elder Coulson came back on the scene, said he had better show himself or the would-be photographer might wait all day. Whereupon the father — the person these birds were accustomed to — busied himself in the garden near the houses, and the martins began to return immediately.

They repeated the experiment several times, and each time the result was the same. When only the relative stranger was sitting close to the house, the martins would not return. When the landlord appeared, they would return without hesitation, even with the stranger still present. The landlord represented security and — maybe — friendship.

There is no need to believe in anthropomorphism — giving human characteristics to martin behavior. Purple martins are not human. They are birds with their own intriguing combination of intelligence traits. They may not be even among the most intelligent of birds, but they are among the most interesting, and like almost any species of wildlife, can develop a real attachment to humans.

Finally, let me suggest that you develop a well balanced motivation for attracting martins. Read as much about them as you can. Talk to other martin landlords. Observe them carefully, using binoculars when possible. Keep a calendar of key dates such as first arrivals and last departures, first nest-building activity, first feeding activity, first fledging, and so on.

In short, learn about martins. You will enjoy them to a much greater extent than if you view them only as "skeeter-eaters."

THREE KEY FACTORS

Three management factors have about equal importance. Neglect one of them and you risk failure. They are (1) house location; (2) house design; and (3) control of nesting problems. All three can be very, very simple.

1. Location

If you do not have a suitable location, there is no need to consider acquiring a house.

For your first house, select the best location your yard offers. This usually means the most open and isolated from vegetation and structures. Do not place under or near trees. Houses should be situated so they can be easily seen and recognized from the air.

At the very least, your house should be 15 feet in all directions from buildings and trees. If surrounded by very tall dense trees, this 30-ft. "cylinder of air" probably will not be enough, and in any situation it helps to have more than the minimum clearance in at least one direction.

If you have choices of open areas, try to select the one in which the main direction of open exposure offers the birds the freest access and the best view of potential food supplies. Martins shy away from houses near trees, and this is traditionally interpreted as a natural fear of predators. However, we think it may also relate to the martin's reliance on flying food.

Martins may simply prefer to nest where they can sit on their houses and have the best view of open air in which insect food may be flying. They do often forage in short flights directly from their houses — somewhat in the manner of flycatchers — although most of their feeding is on longer flights.

While martins do not like to nest near buildings, this can be overemphasized, particularly in the case of human houses. I know of a few successful cases where they have even nested in boxes attached to the walls of human homes.

Locating a house too far from human activity can be just as bad. While making sure your martin house is at least 15 feet from your own house, and preferably farther, make equally sure it is within direct view of your house or at least one area of frequent human activity such as a patio.

If martins have a preference for directions we don't know what it is. Some landlords feel south is the best direction for the main open terrain exposure; west, east and north have their proponents, too. But plenty of successful colonies face every conceivable direction.

Likewise, we can't detect any preference for the direction holes should face. We recommend facing a minimum number of holes into the direction of prevailing winds, so that storm damage can be minimized, but I really don't feel this is a very important factor.

When locating a house, don't overlook adjoining properties as potential open areas. Remember that martins don't recognize property lines. If your yard has a high percentage of tree cover, but your neighbor's is wide open, you may be able to locate your house near the property line and be very successful.

Be sure your neighbor understands the value of these birds and shares your enthusiasm. They will spend more time over his property than yours, and probably eat more of his insects than yours. Everyone should be happy, but make sure he's enthused before taking the step. If the colony is near his bedroom and he likes to sleep late, you could make an enemy instead of a friend.

Also consider the martins already living in your neighborhood. If you can place your house within direct view of occupied martin houses, so much the better. Any new house in a neighborhood may, in effect, be merely another addition to an existing colony and, following their tendency to disperse slightly when they can, a few will probably move into your house the first season.

Water — at least a small pond or stream — is a plus, but that water does not have to be very close. Some authorities feel it must be within 3/4 of a mile. I believe two miles is close enough, but this is academic in most cases. A surprisingly high percentage of homes are within 3/4 of a mile of water.

With exception of flat, sparsely populated regions, ponds exist in surprising numbers — thousands per county — and are often taken for granted. Survey your own community and list every body of water within a one- or two-mile radius. I think you will be satisfied that water is plentiful.

Although martins will fly far to collect mud if necessary, the principal need for water is for drinking and bathing, both of which they do on the wing. Distances of a mile or two are not much to a martin, and nestlings do not need water at all beyond what they get in their food.

Nevertheless, if water is close, that should increase your chances for immediate success. If you can locate your house so that it has a direct view of water, do it, but not at the sacrifice of any other basic location principle. Do not locate close to a tree, for example, just so it can have direct exposure to water.

Martins probably do have preferences in the general types of terrain they hunt over, but they ignore only one type of habitat. They rarely hunt beneath dense tree canopies.

In 1974, Rick Borchelt studied for a week a pair of brooding martins at his family's farm near Cape Girardeau, Missouri. While away from the colony site, these birds spent 45 percent of their time foraging over grassy field habitat including lots of both weeds and grasses; 25 percent in and over forested areas ranging from fairly open woodlots to climax deciduous trees; 15 percent over highway right-of-way covered with tall fescue grass; 5 percent over water; and 10 percent over unaccounted for terrain. Obviously, although they preferred a particular type, they foraged for significant periods over other available habitats as well.

Almost any home has suitable feeding habitat available.

Finally, in selecting a location, study your neighborhood and the approaches to your yard carefully and see if you can notice anything that could discourage — or encourage — martins.

Consider potential nuisances. Don't locate a house near a fire pit or trash burner, for example, since frequent smoke may discourage nesting.

Look for owls and hawks nesting in a neighborhood. They don't always bother a colony, but if you do spot the nesting site of any kind of owl or one of the small hawks, you may be wise to consult a falconer and see if the predator can be forced to nest farther away. Sometimes, that's as simple as plugging a cavity that is preferred by a pair.

When dealing with raptors or any other native birds, always remember that federal law prohibits disrupting their nests without good reason, so consult a licensed falconer or conservation agent to learn what is possible in any specific situation.

Give the needs of the martins priority in your landscaping designs. What looks good to you may not look good to a martin. Modern houses are attractive landscape elements wherever located, but if a conflict does develop, resolve it in favor of the birds. Put that house out there in that open spot even if you would rather have it neatly coordinated in a row of trees or sitting beside a secluded backyard pool.

HOW HIGH?

After deciding where to put it, you must decide how high to mount it. Martins will nest almost equally well at any height in the 8-30-ft. range. I recommend 12-14 feet because it is practical. It is high enough to offer security to birds, and low enough to offer convenience to humans.

In some rare circumstances where low trees prevent an ideal open area at this 12-14-ft. height, but do allow one somewhat higher, it may be advantageous to mount the house on a higher post, but the 12-14-ft. range is satisfactory for nearly all situations.

Finally, you need to decide whether to use a permanent or temporary mount. Most are permanent, with the base of the post sunk in concrete. If you are unsure of your location, however, and want to keep your options open, you can use a "ground socket" at very little cost.

A ground socket is little more than a 2-ft. section of pipe large enough in diameter to snugly accept your mounting post. Set the socket instead of the post into the concrete; then slide the post down into the socket. If you ever decide to move the house, simply lift it from the ground socket and remount it elsewhere.

These are the basics of locating a house to maximize your chances. Now consider the importance of selecting a house that will make it easy for you to handle success.

2. House Design

To be successful under 20th Century conditions, you must manage certain factors — principally nest competitors, parasites and predators. To do this effectively, you need housing designed for convenience.

With modern housing, management is quick and simple. With much traditional housing, it is such a nuisance that it inevitably is neglected, the colony deteriorates, and the martins move on.

With modern housing, many landlords have built flourishing colonies by devoting only a few hours a year to management. With traditional housing, these same techniques would require a few hours a week.

To understand modern design, first let me explain what housing must do for you and the birds today. The following are the functions modern housing must serve.

a. It should be cool. Martins prefer to nest in exposed locations, and this means direct exposure to summer sun. To counteract this, three factors are important: heat reflectiveness, ventilation, and insulating qualities. The first two of these are by far most important.

Color is the primary factor in heat reflectiveness. White and some natural metal finishes are most reflective. Some pastels are next. Far down the line are dark colors, none of which is acceptable for a martin house. Any color can be used for trim, but a dark color should never be used for wall panels or roofing. Bright reds, blues and greens are no more acceptable than black or brown.

Ventilation is the next critical factor. Heated air inside a house rises and must be allowed to escape. Entrance holes by themselves are not adequate; compartments need ventilation holes either in the ceiling or near the tops of the walls. An interior ventilation shaft is an excellent added factor.

Insulation is useful, but not critical. The insulating walls prevent a compartment from heating rapidly, but also from **cooling** rapidly. Without proper reflectiveness and ventilation, insulation cannot overcome a heat problem.

Heat itself can be a serious problem, but most young birds can survive periods up to 100 degrees so long as they are not extended past a few days.

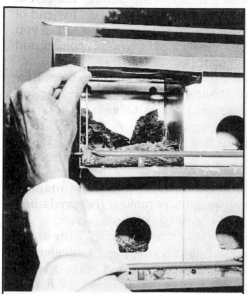

The bright shiny interiors of modern aluminum houses seem as appealing as any other to martins, but not to starlings, which nest in them only rarely. These houses effectively eliminated starlings as nest competitors for martins.

Six of the modern innovations pioneered by the new Trio houses in the '60s are illustrated here. They include lightweight aluminum construction, guard rails, ventilation holes and (top to bottom) easy opening compartments, subfloors for better drainage, and winter door stops.

When combined with parasites, however, the two can become intolerable, drive young birds out of a nest in search of relief, often to the ground below and certain death unless they happen to be rescued by the landlord.

b. It should drain quickly. This seems obvious. Only occasionally will storms blow hard enough to saturate nests in most types of houses, but even one instance can destroy most of the young in an improperly drained house. When compartments have suitable drainage holes in the floor or at the base of the walls or door, or are equipped with subfloors, nests should drain promptly and dry without loss of young.

c. It should protect fledglings. Martins like porches, but these offer no protection for young unless equipped with guard rails or some other type of barrier to prevent unsteady youngsters from toppling off. During final pre-fledging days, young often come out of compartments from time to time. Rails prevent accidents until that final day when each is old enough to launch itself into the world and survive. It is inhumane to erect a house without guard rails.

d. It should discourage starlings. Simplest way is to make certain interiors of compartments are bright and airy. Martins don't mind this, but starlings do. These nest competitors like dark cavities.

e. It should allow control of sparrows. Sometimes these competitors can be discouraged by frequent nest cleanout, so housing should offer an easy way to do this. This means easy raising and lowering, and easy opening of compartments. Housing should also be easy to close up in winter to prevent sparrows from becoming entrenched — and more possessive — during the winter.

f. It should be easily maintained. Housing should be easy to raise and lower vertically so that martin nests need never be disrupted. It should be lightweight and compartments should open easily. Reasons for wanting easy access to nesting compartments include cleanout of sparrow nests, parasite treatment, repairing soaked nests, returning young birds to nests, and keeping scientific records. Fall cleanout is also recommended to increase the life of a house.

It is also desirable to have a finish that does not need frequent repainting, although this job is not objectionable to some persons.

EVALUATION OF EXISTING HOUSING

Now you know the principles of proper housing, so let's evaluate the various types available to you today in terms of how well they meet these criteria.

a. Gourds:

Gourds are, as far as we know, the earliest type of housing used by humans to attract martins. Indians used them in certain eastern and southeastern villages, usually mounting on poles or tree stubs to entice martins to the vicinity of their lodges. They may have valued them as insect-eaters, but the historical references I find are to their value in driving hawks and crows away from food growing or hanging near Indian lodges.

Biggest problems associated with gourds are lack of durability, difficulty in maintenance, and lack of guard rails or predator guards. Operating a gourd-housed colony requires a lot of work.

Typically, a gourd must be painted to have a life expectancy beyond a year. Average life span of a painted gourd is three seasons. As they age they become very dry, lightweight, and vulnerable to storm damage. Entire nests have fallen through the holes broken in gourds during storms.

Maintenance is a problem because of wider distribution of these individual-type compartments. Access to nests is a double problem because there is no convenient way to open them for cleaning or inspection.

No effective way has been devised to rig guard rails or other protective barriers to prevent young from falling out, and I know of no way to rig an owl or crow guard over the entrance to a gourd.

In the past, complaints of young birds on the ground under gourd-housed colonies have been very common.

Mounting costs are relatively higher than for houses because of the wider distribution of the compartments.

b. Wooden houses:

Following gourds, single-compartment wooden houses were erected by European settlers, who gradually began to build larger ones. Purple martins became highly valued on American farms, and almost all of them were housed in large wooden houses of rather plain design, mounted on stationary wooden posts.

House sparrows and starlings were unknown in America during the early centuries and bulky wooden houses were quite adequate. Few other species fought with martins for nesting spaces. If properly located, a house was usually occupied and the colony grew to at least several pairs.

These photos illustrate what too often happens to wooden houses. When neglected, they rapidly deteriorate. The one at right, in Burlington, Iowa, had become home to squirrels. And the ones above once housed a huge colony of martins at Hoyleton, Illinois, but when the owners moved away it was neglected and in a surprisingly short time had been taken over by starlings. (Photo above is by Grover Brinkman, Okawville, Illinois. Photo at right is courtesy the Burlington Hawk Eye.)

Today, wooden houses are still used, but their role has changed. They must be used more discriminatingly now because of the sparrow and starling problem and other factors.

Some elaborate and beautiful examples of craftsmanship adorn the martin house posts of America. Not all of them look as good to martins, however, as they do to human admirers. When properly designed, wooden houses can be effective, but a majority of them are not designed with the birds in mind. If wood is your preference, I urge you especially to study the principles outlined in this chapter, and make certain they are incorporated into your design.

Many wooden house plans available on the market ignore these principles, so simply buying a commercial plan is no guarantee your house will be well designed.

One plan has a "V" roof design that invites water to concentrate at the center of the roof and encourages leaking into the interior.

Many houses are too heavy to raise and lower, can't be opened for cleaning, and are neither well ventilated nor well drained.

Wood is one of the heavier materials used in construction, so you need an effective way of raising and lowering it vertically with some type of mechanical device. Your design should include doors that open, porches with guard rails, ventilation and drainage holes, enough light in compartments to discourage starlings, and a way to close it up in winter. The plan should call for a very light, heat reflective paint color. All of these things should take priority over the beauty of your design. Once they are considered, however, you can design a Taj Mahal replica with solid assurance it will be as good for the birds as it is for you.

c. Masonite houses:

Masonite is as heavy or heavier than most common wood types. One masonite 12-compartment house plan produces a house that weighs more than 50 pounds.

Again, whatever material you use, be sure your design is practical, and you can handle vertical raising and lowering of the finished product.

d. Plastic houses:

Several plastic or fiberglass houses are on the market. All are reasonably lightweight, durable and attractive, and I presume all have compartments at least 6"x6"x6" and suitable for nesting. All designs I have studied have other problems, however.

One very attractive house has a bright red roof, and this is one of the most heat absorptive of all colors, ranking very close to black. This house offers no way to open compartments, so any sparrow nesting material has to be hooked out through entrance holes in the manner of traditional

Lack of durability is a major problem with gourds. Most have to be replaced every two or three years, even if painted. Growing suitable gourds is a hit-and-miss project, and when suitable ones are produced, they must be carefully dried and preserved. Some gourds have broken in bad weather and allowed entire nests to be destroyed. Lack of guard rails or other protection for young is the greatest disadvantage. Allowing young ones to fall to the ground and be eaten by other animals is inhumane and a waste of very beneficial birds.

wooden houses. This type of inconvenience usually discourages a landlord from performing this task enough to discourage sparrows or achieve any other goal.

Any prospective landlord who buys or builds a house only because of its appearance in his yard should leave the holes plugged. It will look better for a much longer number of years; will not contribute to the starling and sparrow population; and will force any prospective martin tenants to move on to housing in which they can flourish and make a bigger contribution to the martin population.

Masonite, like wood, is heavy, making maintenance a problem, and can be too easily remodeled by woodpeckers and squirrels. This house, like virtually every wooden house and plan on the market, has neither guard rails nor any convenient way of cleaning compartments. Wooden and masonite houses must be painted every few years to remain in top condition, and are more attractive to starlings than aluminum houses.

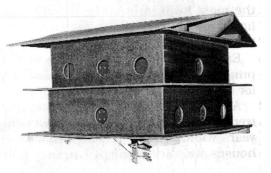

Not all modern houses have adopted the most modern design principles. This compartment could not be opened without destroying a martin nest in it. Those on the top floor could not be opened at all without partially disassembling the floor below them. This same house is held together with a set screw in a plastic collar under the bottom floor. When it starts to wear the entire house can become unstable. This house was also sold without guard rails, as shown here, although some models now have rails.

This plastic house is beautiful, but its roof is an extremely heat-absorbing red, and compartments can be cleaned only by hooking material out through the entrances.

e. Aluminum houses:

Aluminum housing was pioneered in Griggsville, and in my judgment is the most ideal of building materials. Its principle virtue lies in being lightweight enough that a large house can be built that is cool but can still be raised and lowered easily.

Extensive testing proved not only the effectiveness of modern design principles, but also the value of aluminum as the most practical material for incorporating those principles.

Aluminum — either with natural finish or baked-on enamel — is extremely heat reflective. It is very durable and retains its attractiveness for years without maintenance. Starlings do not like to nest in aluminum houses and very rarely do.

Combining these characteristics with design features that can be incorporated into almost any house — ventilation holes, porches and guard rails, easy open doors, etc. — allows construction of the most effective type of housing yet devised. An aluminum house can incorporate every ideal feature and still be lightweight enough for almost anyone of any age to raise and lower easily.

Not all aluminum houses use all these features yet, however, so you should examine carefully before buying.

A house sold by a major catalog house cannot be completely cleaned without disassembling the floors. These floors are pie-shaped, and those in the bottom tier can be easily opened. All contents will fall out, however, so if a compartment contains a martin nest, this feature is not usable.

To open a compartment on the top tier, the lower tier must first be loosened and lowered. To do this, a set screw in a plastic collar at the base of the house must be loosened. This isn't very convenient and, over the long haul, tends to weaken the plastic collar and cause instability of the whole unit. In addition, this house was sold for years without guard rails and some models still do not have protection for young birds.

The aluminum houses developed in Griggsville are so far the only ones using all of the design logic outlined in this chapter. Although this housing is the most advanced to date, this does not mean new things will not be learned tomorrow and new advances made. Nature is not static, and I hope designers of martin housing do not become static in their thinking about nature, either.

OTHER CONSIDERATIONS

Most modern design features are valuable because they help you help the birds. The martins themselves may be attracted to any cavity that is suitably located, even one that ultimately proves too small for brood-raising.

Although many martins have a tendency to nest first in the type of housing they were raised in, they will accept new types quickly. Aluminum housing, a totally new concept less than 25 years ago, was accepted by the martins with surprising speed. In most areas, aluminum houses gained some acceptance the first season, and almost overnight were as effective as any other type in attracting martins.

MOUNTING POSTS

Most mounting posts are made of steel or wood. Some are simple; some are complex arrangements involving boat winches, garage door mechanisms or other mechanical devices for raising and lowering.

Whatever system you use, make certain it will allow your house to raise and lower **vertically** and **easily**. Vertical raising and lowering is essential

A ground socket is a very small investment that can be a very big blessing when a person decides to move a house. When it has been installed in a socket, a post can simply be pulled out of the ground for relocation. An 18-24-inch section of pipe of the correct diameter can be used, but I recommend a commercial ground socket such as the Trio MPS or TGS because these have a clamp at the upper end which prevents a mounting post from rotating inside of it.

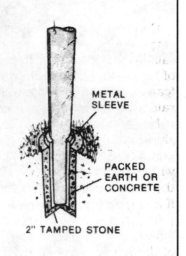

METAL
SLEEVE

PACKED
EARTH OR
CONCRETE

2" TAMPED STONE

Here are just three of the possible ways that a martin installation can be rigged for easy vertical raising and lowering. In two photos, the house slides up and down the pole, controlled in one case by a rope lanyard (operates like a flag) and in the other by a winch and steel cable. In lower example, the post itself telescopes and three sections of galvanized steel pipe slide up and down inside each other, held in the fixed positions by clamps at each joint.

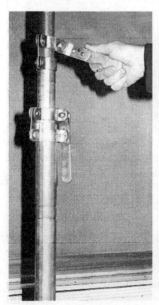
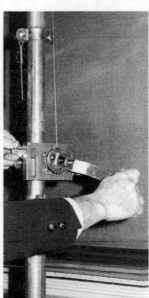
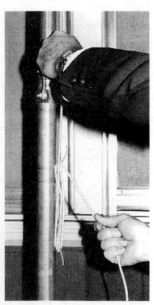

Here is a multiple-house mount that has proved very popular. It was designed by Carl Kurtz of St. Charles, Missouri. Even with the obvious mechanical advantage in this system, the light weight of these aluminum houses makes it much more practical and easy to operate.

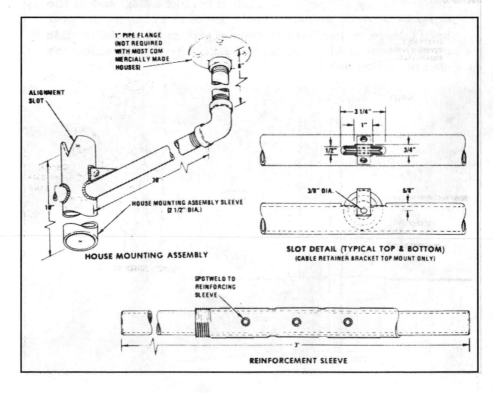

1" PIPE FLANGE (NOT REQUIRED WITH MOST COMMERCIALLY MADE HOUSES)

ALIGNMENT SLOT

HOUSE MOUNTING ASSEMBLY SLEEVE (2 1/2" DIA.)

HOUSE MOUNTING ASSEMBLY

3 1/4"

1"

1/2"

3/4"

3/8" DIA.

5/8"

SLOT DETAIL (TYPICAL TOP & BOTTOM)
(CABLE RETAINER BRACKET TOP MOUNT ONLY)

SPOTWELD TO REINFORCING SLEEVE

3"

REINFORCEMENT SLEEVE

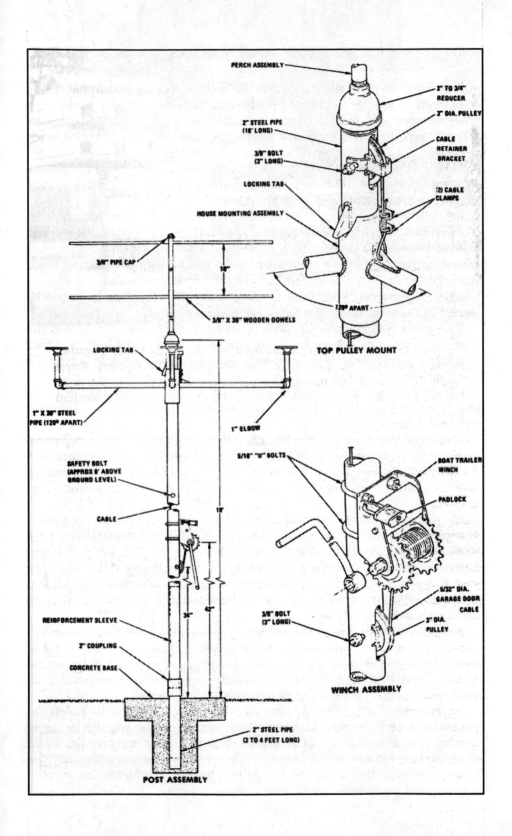

PERCH ASSEMBLY

2" TO 3/4" REDUCER

3" DIA. PULLEY

CABLE RETAINER BRACKET

2" STEEL PIPE (18" LONG)

3/8" BOLT (2" LONG)

(2) CABLE CLAMPS

LOCKING TAB

HOUSE MOUNTING ASSEMBLY

120° APART

TOP PULLEY MOUNT

3/4" PIPE CAP

3/8" X 36" WOODEN DOWELS

18"

LOCKING TAB

1" X 30" STEEL PIPE (120° APART)

1" ELBOW

SAFETY BOLT (APPROX 6' ABOVE GROUND LEVEL)

5/16" "U" BOLTS

BOAT TRAILER WINCH

PADLOCK

CABLE

16'

REINFORCEMENT SLEEVE

2" COUPLING

CONCRETE BASE

36"

42"

3/8" BOLT (3" LONG)

5/32" DIA. GARAGE DOOR CABLE

3" DIA. PULLEY

WINCH ASSEMBLY

2" STEEL PIPE (3 TO 4 FEET LONG)

POST ASSEMBLY

so that you can manage your colony without destroying martin nests that may be in it. Traditional hinged posts that "lay over" are not practical in this era when you may need to tear out sparrow nests, or add parasite killer, or replace young birds in a nest — or when you may simply want to keep track of the progress of your martin families.

Most modern systems are available with raising and lowering systems ranging from simple telescoping posts to integrated systems that use rope or steel cable to raise and lower the house.

Prior to 20 years ago the great majority of mounts were simply fixed wooden posts, usually 4"x4" or larger. On those rare occasions when a landlord wanted to reach a house, he used a ladder. When he wanted to remove something from a compartment he used a wire and hooked it out through the entrance hole. Times have changed.

Most commercial houses in use today are Trio models. It would be useful to mention a few tips for using those systems.

When mounting a rope- or cable-operated system, orient it so that the winch or rope bracket is on the same side of the post as the sun. This way you will not be looking up into the sun when you lower a house during the middle hours of the day.

If you mount a sparrow trap on your post, mount it on the opposite side from the rope bracket and position the trap bracket so it does not interfere with operating the house.

Additional perching space is always beneficial. Nature House makes an auxiliary perch that works on both the TW-12 system and MPQ and MP-14 telescoping posts. And if you are a creative person you can use wooden dowels or steel rods to adapt a variety of perch extensions to your Trio houses.

But remember, when buying or building auxiliary perches, they must always be mounted on the houses themselves, with the exceptions of those models mentioned above (TW-12, MPQ, MP-14). The TW-12 has a steel sleeve extending below the house which moves up and down with the house. A perch can be mounted on that sleeve. And, of course, a perch can be mounted on the top section of any telescoping post since it moves up and down with the house, too.

A couple of safety notes: The cable winches on both the Trio Castle and Trio Wade systems have safety catches which prevent either of these houses from accidentally falling out of control. It also prevents the crank handle from whirling around and striking a person's wrist if his hand accidentally slips off the crank while raising the house.

Nevertheless, it's wise to operate this winch assembly carefully, especially when lowering the house. During that phase, you will be using one hand to release that safety catch while the other one cranks. While either of these houses can be raised and lowered by a person using only one finger to release the safety catch and two fingers to operate the crank, I recommend using both hands and reasonable care.

Many enthusiasts feel strongly that auxiliary perching space increases the appeal of their site, and I agree. Utility wires nearby are almost always a plus-factor. This photo shows a "tree" that Raleigh Stotz had made using three Trio MHP-1 perches.

I also recommend use of the TG-12LL lanyard lock that is available for the Trio Grandpa. This inexpensive accessory fits on the bottom of the house around the pole and prevents a TG-12 from falling accidentally. If a rope slips out of the landlord's hand, the house will stop instantly, regardless of where it is on the post.

This locking device would probably allow you to maintain your house at any alternative height on the post if you wanted to experiment with lower heights, but I don't recommend this. First, the device might allow gradual slippage down the post over a long period of time, and second, it would not prevent wind from causing a house to rotate somewhat on the post. This could disorient birds nesting in the house, and cause their failure to feed young for an indeterminate period.

Some other good advice: Use the safety clamp on any other safety equipment provided with the system you purchase. The safety clamps should be fixed at a level just above the height of the tallest person using the system. When you lower the house drop the clamp out of the way. After you raise the system, return the clamp to the proper height. An extra margin of safety is always worth the effort.

Workers at Purple Martin Junction appreciate convenient raising and lowering systems even more than most landlords because the Junction has 40 houses, almost all of which have martins nesting in them each year. Usually 36 or 37 houses are occupied.

3. *Problem Control*

Don't be intimidated by the size of this section. All of the management performed each year by the typical landlord does not require more than a total of a few hours.

While success requires only a little of the modern landlord's time, this is partially because he already knows most of what is in this chapter. He doesn't have to spend many hours groping for answers to new questions or old problems.

Every species of life has its own peculiar set of problems, and nature equips each to handle those problems, at least well enough to survive as a species. As the balance of nature changes — whether due to the infinitely shifting interplay of species themselves, or to the spread of human civilization — stresses upon some species increase. They adjust, or they die out. Countless thousands of species have flourished and then become extinct since the dawn of time.

Pressures have increased on purple martins during the past 100 years, but they have survived, possibly because all of humanity's attempts to eradicate insect populations have proved futile. Flying insect food still abounds.

Martins are fortunate in some respects. The South American rain forest situation is an example. Tens of thousands of acres of that forest, where millions of birds winter, is disappearing each year as chain saws and bulldozers advance. Some highly specialized species are already beginning to decline because of loss of winter food sources.

The broad spectrum insect diet of martins and other swallows makes these birds less vulnerable to this particular threat. They have other stresses, however, and you can help your own success by helping alleviate them.

Here are my recommendations for controlling the major problems. All are important, but I rate them in this descending order of importance: (a) starlings and sparrows; (b) parasites; (c) predators; (d) weather; (e) miscellaneous.

STARLINGS AND SPARROWS

Every case of both rapid and steady growth I can think of has been accompanied by rigid elimination of house sparrows and starlings. By rapid and steady I mean projects in which numbers have shown a healthy jump each year until martins total at least 40-50 pairs within 4-5 years.

Even though house sparrows will co-exist with martins after an initial period of rivalry, the existence of only a pair or two in each house seems to slow the growth of a colony drastically — or stop it altogether.

Only one pair of starlings can prevent an entire house from being used by martins, but starlings are much easier to deal with, as you will see.

Bait-type traps, like this Trio ST-1, are effective year around, and more effective in winter than nest-type traps. Fresh, white bread is usually the only bait needed. After a bird is caught, it will quickly find its way into the central holding compartment and the trap can be reset. Food and water should be kept available to those sparrows in the central compartment.

A nesting cavity can be turned into a house sparrow trap that needs no bait because sparrows have an incessant tendency to investigate potential nest cavities, even when they are already established in a cavity. This Trio SD-1 was designed to replace any door in any Trio house and turn that compartment into a temporary trap. When a sparrow steps on a trigger inside, it releases a bar which drops across the door opening. Included with it is a removal device (below) which allows the landlord to release the sparrow into a plastic bag, and the trap can be reset without opening the compartment.

I suggest two levels of control techniques for starlings and sparrows. The first includes "starling-proofing" your houses and using nest cleanout to discourage sparrows. Here's what I mean:

To prevent starlings from nesting in your houses, use bright, airy interiors. If you use aluminum houses, this has already been taken care of. If you use wood or some other type of houses, either paint the interiors white or line them with reflective sheet aluminum. At least paint or "aluminumize" the back wall opposite the entrance hole. This one receives most of the light entering the compartment and by itself can brighten the cavity considerably.

Metal foil may also work but it tends to work loose more easily than sheet aluminum.

I recommend only white paint. Aluminum paint will not achieve the desired result; may actually darken a wall.

To discourage house sparrows, remove their nests at least once a week, preferably more often. Burn this material each time or make it inaccessible, because otherwise the sparrows will simply replace it in the cavity — and do so in an amazingly short time.

Some landlords prefer to allow the sparrows to lay eggs, then replace those eggs with pebbles, marbles or some other "look-alike" eggs and allow the sparrow to brood them, unsuccessfully of course. But I much prefer to try to cause the sparrows to go elsewhere to nest, because their presence in a colony seems to curtail its growth.

Some sparrows are easily discouraged; some are not and seem so persistent they will continue trying to nest indefinitely. In these cases, you will have to resort to another tactic.

In addition, I recommend stopping sparrow cleanout while martins are brooding their own eggs. Although these incidents are only occasional, a sparrow whose nest has been destroyed will sometime retaliate against a neighboring martin pair. Fighting will break out for a brief time. Sometimes martin nests are destroyed during the day or so following destruction of a sparrow nest, and in a few cases circumstantial evidence points to the sparrows as the culprits.

So what do you do in the cases of sparrows that will not become discouraged? Go to the second level of strategy.

The second level involves trapping.

Both starlings and house sparrows are imported species and not protected by native bird laws. Either can be trapped and handled in any way the landlord chooses. How you do handle this problem depends on your own values and your attitude toward these two species.

The late Dr. T. E. Musselman, who was one of the nation's best known naturalists for many years, was among the most militant on the subject of sparrow elimination. He believed strongly that their numbers must be reduced in order to bring back not only martins but many other native species to all kinds of homes and neighborhoods. He conducted an experimental program in which he rigidly eliminated sparrows and starlings from his neighborhood and then after only two seasons recorded several species of woodpeckers, thrushes, warblers and swallows beginning to nest in that neighborhood again.

Dr. Musselman listed these legal options available to persons wanting to remove the two problem species from a yard:

You can shoot them if your home is not within a municipality that restricts firearms use.

You can trap and transport them away. To make sure they don't return you will need to take them at least 15 miles. House sparrows stick close to home. When released within three miles of home, nearly 100 percent will return, but that percentage decreases as the distance increases. At 15 miles, very few return. Starlings are more freewheeling, and 15 miles may not be a safe distance to guarantee their not returning.

For most persons who elect to transport them away, this means a way is needed to accumulate a number sufficient to justify a trip of that length.

You can accumulate birds in either a large cardboard box or a cage made of wire mesh, but be sure to keep them supplied with food and water. Whatever type of large container is used, it should fit easily into your car or whatever conveyance you use to transport them out of the area.

One other factor in using this practice: Some persons may resent your releasing these birds in their neighborhood. If you consider them a problem, the new hosts may not like the idea any better.

Finally, you can trap and destroy them. T. E. listed these as the most common methods used: (a) a sharp, 180-degree twist of the head, breaking the neck; (b) a sharp rap on the back of the head; (c) drowning; and (d) suffocation by carbon monoxide. The last method, presumed to be the most painless, is done by placing the birds in a large bag, introducing only a whiff of automobile exhaust, and immediately reclosing the bag. Birds have very low tolerance to carbon monoxide and death occurs quietly.

Two types of traps are available, and each serves a specific purpose.

Bait-type traps like the Trio ST-1 or Havahart are effective year around, and sometimes used in winter as well to remove sparrows from backyard bird feeding stations. Fresh bread is very effective in attracting sparrows.

Many persons who do extensive trapping say results are much greater when one or two sparrows are allowed to remain inside the trap as decoys. Other sparrows are attracted more quickly. When using decoys make certain food and water are available to them at all times.

The second type of trap is used in the birdhouse itself, and is extremely effective at catching the sparrows that are actually causing problems in the house. Traps like the Trio SD-1 resemble a regular Trio door and are easily interchanged with a door to convert that nesting compartment into a trap. House sparrows continually investigate potential nesting cavities, even while they are nesting successfully, and this curiosity causes them to be quickly trapped even though no bait is used.

House sparrow (left) and purple martin eggs are easy to distinguish. Those of the sparrow are speckled with brown; those of the martin are white. Those of the starling are light greenish-blue.

Quickest results, of course, will usually be achieved by putting the trap in the compartment you have just cleaned a sparrow nest from.

This type of trap has an entrance hole large enough for sparrows but too small for mature martins to enter. Since house sparrows are the only small birds normally seen on martin houses during the nesting season, other species are rarely caught. Even so, be sure to monitor your house frequently when using this type of trap.

While many trappers catch starlings, too, in the bait-type traps, totals are nearly always much lower than those for sparrows. If you **have** large numbers of starlings, however, you can **catch** large numbers of starlings. Sometimes huge numbers. To do this, you need a large, cage-type trap that can be baited with grain and is large enough to accumulate dozens of these birds before being emptied. You will probably need to have this sort of trap specially built for you, and may not want to bother with this unless you are a farmer or other food producer suffering big economic losses to big flocks of starlings.

Whatever type of trapping program you are using, I urge you to remember these things:

1. House sparrows, starlings and wild pigeons are the only common species you can legally trap. That's because they are species not native to this continent. Fortunately, very few other birds will wander into these

This series shows the progressive construction of a house sparrow's nest. The initial layer may resemble a martin nest, but material quickly starts up both sides of the cavity. The compartment is soon filled, leaving only a tunnel through the center to a small nest chamber in the back of this mass of material. This entire construction can take place in less than two days' time.

traps, but it does happen and you must be able to identify the trappable species.

Grackles are a native species not popular with many bird enthusiasts. These will occasionally get into a sparrow trap — and quite often get into the big starling traps mentioned above. Grackles can now be killed if they are a nuisance, but be sure to contact a game agent before doing this.

You are not apt to confuse a male house sparrow — it has a bold black face mask — with any other species, but the female is a rather plain looking bird and at a glance could be confused with some of our native sparrows. I suggest buying a low cost bird guide such as **Birds of North America** (Golden Press) and keeping it handy. You will rarely trap any kind of native sparrow around your martin colony, but it is wise to know what you are looking at.

2. In addition to knowing your backyard birds, be sure you know what is happening at your trap whenever it is open. Monitor your trap conscientiously. Release protected species immediately. Keep food and water in the trap at all times that a bird is being confined. Don't allow birds to hurt themselves. If you happen to have both starlings and sparrows in a

If tree swallows or bluebirds are keeping martins from moving into your house, try erecting single-cavity houses in the area as an alternative. Since both these species usually arrive a bit earlier than martins and start nesting earlier, they may move into the new housing if your martin house is still closed when they arrive. The tree swallow and bluebird houses above are on the farm of Joe Goodman at Masonville, Michigan. Photo is by the Gladstone Delta Reporter.

trap at the same time, make sure they are not fighting and injuring each other. In short, when you operate a trap, do it humanely.

OTHER COMPETITORS

Tree swallows are pretty little birds that nest in loosely scattered colonies across the countryside, preferably near water. They often nest in bluebird houses as well as natural cavities, and two pairs seldom nest very close to each other. One pair, however, can take over an entire house and keep other species out.

"Even though the martins obviously wanted to nest, the tree swallows kept driving them away," is a complaint we hear occasionally.

Here's what I recommend: Erect one or two single-cavity houses at other locations on your property and keep your martin house closed each spring until martins actually arrive. Keep every other species from moving into the single-cavity houses, and hope that a pair of tree swallows will move into one of them.

Since tree swallows can survive on food gleaned from trees or bushes, they can arrive in an area slightly earlier than martins, and often do. Consequently, they may show interest in one of the small houses before you have to open your martin house. When this happens, your battle should be won and you can enjoy both species nesting near your home.

When **bluebirds** were more plentiful, they occasionally took over a martin house in the same way and kept martins from nesting in it, but bluebirds are so rare now, especially in the human environs preferred by martins, this problem would be an oddity.

Great crested flycatchers have nested in martin houses, but this isn't very common, either. This is a woodland bird and usually does not pick open locations like those of most martin houses. In a pinch, however, they will nest anywhere, even in a mailbox.

Trademark of a great crested flycatcher nest is the presence of a dry snakeskin. Most nests have one. The bird itself is brownish, with yellow underneath, rusty tail, and neat topknot. These birds are usually popular, too, with humans, but if you want to discourage them I suspect cleaning out their nest a time or two will do it.

Wrens may nest in martin houses, too. If so, clean out their nests (each pair usually starts more than one nest), and put up more suitable houses for them elsewhere in the yard. Erect these houses as far from the martin house as possible, because wrens — like starlings, house sparrows, blue jays and maybe a few other species — may raid martin nests, puncturing eggs and throwing them from the house.

b. Parasites:

This is the second most serious problem, but control is simple. There are dozens of tiny species that can parasitize your martins, but most problems will involve only nest mites, fleas or blowflies. Control is the same.

First, select a parasiticide. Second, apply it at the beginning of each season and again in each compartment after young have hatched in that compartment.

If properly applied, any of the commonly used substances will be effective. These include sulfur, which has been popular with martin landlords for generations; various commercial chemicals; and a non-chemical material called diatomaceous earth.

I prefer diatomaceous earth because I don't have to worry about subtle, unknown side effects it may have on the birds themselves. This is a powder made from fossilized diatoms, tiny water creatures whose crystallized remains were deposited in beds over the ages. These crystals have microscopic, razor-sharp edges. When an insect — whether a pinpoint-sized mite or something as large as a cockroach — crawls over it, these edges lacerate the skin and within hours the insect dehydrates and dies.

Diatomaceous earth (we call it D.E. for short) is, however, so soft to a human's touch it can be eaten. It is added to certain animal feeds to prevent caking.

Two types are available. Commercial roach-killers like "Dead End" are made from fresh water diatoms. A substance used in filtration systems of swimming pools is made from salt water diatoms and isn't as effective as insect-killer. The edges of salt water crystals are not as sharp as those of fresh water diatoms.

Commercial chemicals often used in martin houses include carbaryl (Sevin), rotenone, pyrethrins, malathion and nicotine (Black Flag and others). Sevin has become popular in recent years, but I should point out that use of this product is technically not legal in a wild bird's nest. Chemicals can be used only for purposes specifically approved by federal regulatory agencies, and approved uses are listed on labels. Wild bird nests aren't listed for Sevin.

Other naturally occurring substances have been used in various regions. Cedar chips and tobacco stems are most often recommended. In tests at Purple Martin Junction, cedar chips did not work very well, but tobacco did seem reasonably effective. I suspect it is one of the most useful of the "natural" treatments. Nicotine, in fact, is a major component of some commercial insecticides.

The Nature Society tested parasiticides at Purple Martin Junction in 1982 and 1983, and found that when a substance is applied is more important than which substance is used. The Society concluded that nests should be treated twice during each season — once at the beginning and a second time shortly after the eggs hatch.

Further, it is recommended that if a landlord could treat only once, the mid-season treatment is far more important. It spoke favorably of diatomaceous earth because it is safe and is "effective enough." (D.E. actually finished third in effectiveness behind Sevin and sulfur, but the three were so close the differences were given no biological significance.)

Reason for treating twice is that most substances lose their effectiveness after a few weeks, at about the time some types of parasites are becoming active.

To apply control substance:

If your house has subfloors, dust the substance liberally under them. The mid-season treatment should be dusted on top of the nests as well, generally around the edges. Do not dust material directly on nestlings, especially near the eyes and mouth parts.

Use two tablespoonfuls of either diatomaceous earth or sulfur. Use one tablespoonful of the more potent chemicals mentioned above. Be very sure you read and follow instructions on the label of any chemical you use.

Another note of caution: don't get any of these materials in your eyes or inhale them. If you work with large numbers of nests, wear a face mask, not only in applying pesticides, but at other times in the season when working with dry nesting materials.

Blackflies, or "buffalo gnats," can cause severe problems by attacking young in the nests. A repellent named Flys Away II has reportedly been very effective at keeping them away. Blackflies are not a common problem, however, and spraying frequently all season long for a problem that probably won't happen would not be very practical.

I recommend watching for unusual swarms of any kinds of gnats in the vicinity of your yard. If such an outbreak occurs, then spray your house thoroughly.

Any pesticide powder should be thoroughly scattered so that birds cannot eat it. Do not leave in exposed piles as illustrated here. Ideally, it should be deposited under a subfloor. In one well documented case, purple martins ate a mixture of sulfur and EPN that had been left in little piles on the floors — and died.

c. Predators:

You may never achieve 100 percent control of predator problems, but you can come very close simply by controlling access to your houses. If you live close to a forest, you can never totally insure against one of the small, fast woodland hawks — Cooper's or sharp-shinned — surprising one of your martins around the colony site, but you can control other types of predation.

Even the small fast hawks cannot catch a martin in open flight, but they can sometimes catch them off guard around the colony site. If you are one of the few landlords who have this problem, a falconer in your area may be able to suggest a solution to it.

Very few landlords have all the common potential predators in their vicinity. Some have none at all. For the average landlord, however, some predation possibility exists so it is best to be aware of how to control it.

Snakes can be prevented from reaching houses by fitting each post with a snake guard. Most common type is an inverted cone made of sheet metal. A local metal worker can make one for you quickly.

Radius from the post should be 18 inches, and the lower edge of the cone should be at least 30 inches above the ground. If bolts are used to join the seam, the projecting ends should be on the top side rather than the bottom. This may not be as neat, but it won't give a snake anything to grip on the underside of the cone.

Mount the cone below the lowest joint of your telescoping post so it does not interfere with operation of the post.

Any ground predator can climb a wooden post and some can climb steel posts. We have a few cases on record of **raccoons** successfully climbing 1-3/4" steel posts. This is very unusual, but you should be aware it can happen.

The conical snake guard mentioned above will thwart raccoons and other ground predators as well.

Although **squirrels** are not thought of as predators, they have killed young martins, and have taken over wooden houses for nesting sites, so make sure they can't reach your house, either. Since most houses are located well away from trees, this should be no problem, but be sure the nearest utility wires are not close enough for squirrels to jump from a wire to a house.

Cats are not good at climbing steel posts, but they can jump surprisingly well — as much as six feet vertically — so be sure they cannot reach a house from a rooftop or other structure directly below the house.

Main danger from cats is to young martins that fall to the ground in late summer. If yours is a house cat, make sure that's where it is throughout the summer. Also keep an eye out for other cats prowling the neighborhood. With modern houses having guard rails, you won't often find a

The predator guard on this wood duck house photographed by George Esler could be climbed by a large snake. We recommend a wider one such as the flattened cone on this backyard installation belonging to Dick Palmer of Lynn Haven, Florida. It has 18-inch radius with 4-inch slope, and should be able to deter the largest of snakes.

young martin on the ground, but it is possible, and even one martin is too many to lose unnecessarily.

Owls are among the most important of martin predators. In most regions, **great horned owls** and **screech owls** are worst offenders, but **barred** and **barn owls** also can take a toll.

Great horned owls are so large they have been known to tear doors off houses, but little screech owls can be just as big a problem. Once started, an owl may return to a colony several times, sometimes taking several birds in just one raid.

In some cases, it may be possible to remove a problem owl from your neighborhood, but do not undertake this yourself. Contact a falconer who is familiar with the law. Moving the owl out of the area may be possible in a given case, but even if it is, it takes a trained person.

A far better solution, whenever it is possible, is to owl-proof your house. We have had several reports from landlords who say they have had good success with homemade owl-and-crow guards that were easy to rig.

With a house having porches, this can be done by cutting sheets of plastic coated "hardware cloth" to fit over the face of the house, using

Modern houses with porches can be easily adapted with owl or crow guards made of plastic coated hardware cloth. R. W. Johnson of Winter Haven, Florida, who had a problem with fish crows, fortified his Castle very effectively using 1/4-inch hardware cloth and 3/8-inch dowel pins. Martins did not hesitate to accept the new set-up. Heavy vertical wires have also been used successfully.

wire or screws to anchor the hardware cloth to the porches. Cut new entrance holes large enough to admit martins but not large enough for the big predatory birds. This has the effect of extending the depth of the entrance hole by as much as the depth of the porch.

Another option is to use heavy wire or dowel rods, fixed vertically to the edge of the porches at approximately 2-1/2-inch intervals. This has the same effect of keeping large birds away from the regular entrance holes.

These types of guards keep out both owls and crows, and present a little greater challenge for smaller birds like blue jays and grackles.

Crows can wreak havoc on a colony, but seldom do, mainly because most martin houses are located near human homes and crows are much too wary to venture there.

You may want to wait until martins are brooding eggs before attaching these guards. This will insure the resident martins won't become discouraged themselves and move elsewhere.

If your colony is raided and you aren't sure what did it, examine both the house, the ground below it, and other parts of your yard. Snakes are usually the cleanest type of predator in that they do not tear feathers from their victims, but swallow them whole. Although frightened birds scrambling to escape may lose some feathers, a house that has been raided by a snake is quite often completely free of evidence.

Both owls and ground predators like raccoons may leave feathers or other evidence in a nest, and may scatter the nest itself. Sometimes it is difficult to tell which type of predator was there.

Owls sometimes leave other evidence, however. After eating, owls often cough up pellets of feathers and other undigestible parts. Traces of these materials may be on the ground under the house or under a nearby tree where they take victims to eat them.

Also, if the raid occurs in wet weather, telltale evidence may be much more obvious. Look for muddy paw prints on the house or pole. If there is none, and should be, chances are the raider came through the air.

Over the years, you may experience minor loss of eggs or young to raids by starlings, wrens, blue jays, house sparrows, or other species of small birds. You can do something about the starling and sparrow culprits, but you are limited in what you can do about the others. They are native, protected species. In most cases, they are favorites, too, and you would not hurt them if you could.

The occasional damage they do is part of the normal functioning of nature and a little bit of this you should tolerate. Fortunately, these species rarely present a serious or continuing threat to a colony or its growth.

d. Weather:

Weather problems come in three forms:

First are spring cold snaps of at least 3-4 days. When the temperature dips to the low 40s, insects stop flying and the martins' food supply disappears. Most early arriving martins can survive 3-4 days without food, even though migration may have used up their fat reserves. After that, they deteriorate very rapidly.

My advice: Watch them carefully. Whenever a martin cannot or will not fly away when you approach, it is in trouble and you should capture it and move it into a warmer place. A large, closed cardboard box will be suitable since they will not injure themselves flying around inside it after they revive.

I suggest not putting the box and birds in a room that is more than moderately warm. Being warmed too quickly can be a shock, too.

You will need to feed each bird every hour or two. Although martins will learn to pick up food for themselves after a time, you will normally have these "cold snap" victims only a couple of days and during that short time you will have to force feed them. The subject of what to feed and how to feed it is handled in much more detail in chapter 11.

As soon as the weather breaks and temperatures seem certain to remain above the mid-40s, release the martins as soon as they are able to fly. Recovery should be quick.

During extreme cold weather, martins sometimes pack into a single compartment. We have found 12-15 in a single 6"x6"x6" compartment and have had reports ranging as high as 29 in one room. This sharing of body heat seems to help survival, and I suspect a modified form of hibernation is also operating, with body functions slowed much as swifts are known to do.

If the cold has persisted for only a day or two, leave them alone, but after that it is a judgment call. You may save them by taking them out of a packed compartment and into a warmer area. On the other hand, you may simply startle them into flying away and if they do not have the energy or motivation to reassemble, they may then simply die more quickly scattered throughout the neighborhood.

Second weather problem occurs when cold rains are accompanied by hard winds. This can soak nests so severely that many young are lost through the combination of cold and moisture. This was the condition that caused widespread devastation of colonies in 1972 when Hurricane Agnes swept through the Middle Atlantic states.

Best thing you can do for your martins if this occurs is make sure they have dry nests. If it is obvious the nests will not dry out quickly, replace them. Here's how:

Collect a supply of dry material such as straw or twigs. Armed with this, repair one nest at a time. Gently remove the eggs or young from the nest, scrape out everything in the compartment, place a pad of fresh, dry materials on the floor, retreat the nest with parasiticide, replace the eggs or young and close the compartment.

When parents are lost — for any reason — you can raise the young if you have time for it. Follow feeding instructions in chapter 11.

Young birds soon learn to open their mouths and grab food when offered. Sometimes they even learn to pick up food laid in front of them and feeding becomes as simple as with any other species.

Third weather complication involves tornadoes or other serious windstorms. We occasionally hear of storms destroying houses and nests, or killing parent birds. About all you can do is examine your colony after a severe storm and see if any survivors need your help.

I am pleased to point out that the aluminum houses made in Griggsville have an extraordinary record of surviving storms. Not always — sometimes they suffer extreme damage like everything else — but in a surprising number of cases they come through without any damage at all.

We have pictures of Trio houses standing unscathed in scenes of otherwise total devastation in Florida, Texas, Missouri and Illinois, and numerous letters reporting similar occurrences. It's either a tribute to the engineering in these modern houses, or to the unpredictable behavior of these most violent of storms.

e. Miscellaneous problems:

Kids with BB guns and vandalism both fall into the same category of problem — ignorance-related.

Vandalism in backyards is rare; it is more common at vacation retreats, parks or other locations visited only occasionally. Likewise the shooting of martins directly off houses in a yard is rare, but losses in the general vicinity of a yard may not be so rare. Children often cannot distinguish among bird species, and those who set out to shoot "sparrows" may shoot at anything that will sit still — including martins perched on wires or TV antennas in your neighborhood.

Best chance for curing either of these problems is to get the word around among neighbors that you have a colony of martins. Explain why you like these birds and what they do for the neighborhood. Make sure the "opinion-molders" in your neighborhood get the word and capture some of your enthusiasm. These are the people others look to for leadership and approval of anything new.

Identify the kids most apt to be out shooting birds and make a point to talk to them about your birds. Don't assume they will be indifferent. I think most kids will make a point not to shoot martins if they know the birds are important to someone. Most ignorance among children comes from indifference among adults. When no one talks to them much about different birds, they are naturally not very discriminating when they get a chance to shoot at something. This does not mean that many of them cannot be quickly persuaded to care. Don't presume the worst.

If this doesn't work, try talking to their parents. If that doesn't work, talk to a law enforcement agent. In some cases a city policeman will be most effective; in others a game agent. Success has a lot to do with the personalities involved.

You will not always get the satisfaction you expect even from a game agent, because some game agents do not list nongame species among their priorities. But state conservation departments and the law enforcement agents — both state and federal — associated with them are steadily changing. Emphasis on nongame wildlife is growing rapidly, and that's good. Every day it increases your chances of finding a sympathetic ear when you take a genuine problem to a law enforcement agent.

Fortunately, most martin enthusiasts never encounter this problem. Most colonies are located close to human homes and this acts as a natural control over other humans looking for casual mischief.

Pesticides can cause losses, but this subject is so complex it can't be treated in a few paragraphs. Fortunately, large scale losses are not often reported.

If you do have a sudden unexplained loss of a large number of birds, both poisoning and disease are possible causes. First take a couple specimens to a veterinarian to see if he can determine the cause. If a disease, he most likely can identify that.

If the vet says it is an obvious or suspected case of poisoning, and you have a large number of specimens to examine (at least a dozen), contact a local conservation department or university extension agent and ask whether your state has a service available to analyze them. (The vet may have this information, too.) This is an expensive process, but some cases are accepted by state universities or other agencies if enough specimens are available to provide evidence that the poison, if it can be identified, is a serious threat.

Loss of an occasional bird or two probably won't be considered a serious problem. Sudden massive kills may be.

4. More good ideas:

Here are some other ideas that may increase your success.

a. Eggshells:

Although martins normally will not eat from a feeder, they will eat eggshells. Some authorities feel this is to correct a mineral deficiency associated with their own egg-laying; others feel it is used as grit. Whatever the reason, most martins are attracted to eggshells, and once they discover a source, colonies will consume them eagerly.

Females are the biggest users. Shells are eaten by adults and also fed to young. A feeder usually attracts their attention quicker, is more convenient, and makes for easier viewing, but the birds will pick them up from the ground or any other surface.

Save your shells from normal kitchen use and store in zip-lock refrigerator bags until needed. Break into pieces the size of small fingernails. Dry in normal air or for 2-3 hours spread on cookie sheets in a low-heat oven.

Put them out early in the nest-building period. Once the martins start using them, keep the feeder well supplied.

Some persons say offering shells seems to have made the difference in first attracting martins, but these cases may be coincidental. It's definite, though, that offering shells will make your yard more popular with the martins already there.

b. Convenience nesting materials:

Martins probably produce more of both eggs and young, and raise healthier families, if they do not have to use a great deal of energy in nest-building. You can help in this regard simply by making it easy for them to build.

At the first sign of nest-building interest, put a supply of suitable materials in a conspicuous place in your yard, and keep it well supplied throughout the period in which your martins are building nests. This may stretch over several weeks, depending on the size of your colony. Nest-building is a casual affair with some martins and may stretch over a two-week period for an individual pair.

Chances are your supplies will shorten that period considerably, and enable your birds to get started laying at earlier dates.

Don't forget mud. Some colonies use very little mud, but nearly all pairs use at least a little. Use a hose or buckets of water to create a small mud puddle somewhere in your yard or garden. It need be no more than a foot or two in diameter. Check it every day to make sure it is moist, and dampen it periodically.

Put both mud and stick supplies in open locations so martins landing there will be safe from lurking predators.

Nest-building materials should be cut into convenient lengths of 4-6 inches. Materials such as straw, string, twine, twigs, strips of corn stalk, etc., make good nest items.

Grasses may not be good items to offer. Although a few martins build nests carefully crafted of fine grass, these may offer a better environment for certain parasites. I recommend offering somewhat bulkier items like twigs or straw.

Again, free nest-building materials may not help start a colony in your yard, but they can add to the success of the martins already there.

c. Taped chatter:

Playing recorded sounds of purple martins in your yard will usually attract martins. In some cases the birds have stayed to nest, although it hasn't been proved conclusively that this was the cause.

Whether a tape attracts nesters or not, it can be a very entertaining addition to your martin program. Some persons who had not seen martins in their neighborhood previously have been surprised when martins showed up to investigate within minutes after recorded chatter began playing on a loudspeaker, stereo or "ghetto-blaster" in their yards.

If you have a friend with martins, you may be able to tape some of the activity at his colony. Early season chatter is probably more effective. Avoid alarm or distress calls. These will attract attention, too, but your chances will be better if martins don't associate your yard only with alarm calls.

If you have no local source, you can purchase a copy of Dr. J. W. Hardy's "Sounds of Purple Martins" cassette tape or compact disc. It can be obtained from Nature Society, Purple Martin Junction, P.O. Box 390, Griggsville, IL 62340-0390.

Play the tape either in your yard or at an open window near the yard. Turn the volume up high. If your first effort brings no results, try it again several times during the day — early morning, mid-morning, mid-afternoon, evening.

Good luck.

On July 26, 1969, a young purple martin attached itself to the Salina, Kansas, Silver Sabres marching band while it was practicing in Hutchinson. It refused to leave the group, returning repeatedly to the drum section where it would perch on a drum stick — even while the stick was in use. So the band took the bird home to Salina, took turns feeding it until it finally decided it should become a wild bird. "Silver," who definitely marched to a different drummer, presumably migrated.

Chapter 11

Emergency Care

Hundreds, perhaps thousands, of purple martins are rescued each year by concerned landlords and saved from cold, starvation or injury. The most common request we have is for information on hand-feeding young martins. Proceeding correctly, you can enjoy a high percentage of success. Here's how:

1. Attempt to hand-feed a young martin only after you see no possibility that it can be returned to its parents or to another pair of martins feeding young that are as near as available to its age. Foster parents won't always accept a newcomer of a different age, but they do so often enough that it's worth a try. If the bird is rejected, it won't be fed, and will probably be back on the ground in a short time.

2. Keep orphaned or injured birds in a moderately warm, dry place where they cannot injure themselves. A cardboard box is suitable, especially in the case of injured birds that need to be kept immobilized. This is easier to do in a box that can be kept darkened inside.

If you decide to have a martin as a house guest for a few days or few weeks, be aware that accidents can happen. Keep in mind that birds can fall prey to vacuum cleaners, toilets and other open water, stoves, pots of cooking food, cats, dogs, kids, aerosol sprays, and numerous other things we take for granted around a house. If a young bird is to be released to the wild, don't let it lose its fear of your cat or dog, no matter how harmless your pets may be. Those the bird will meet in the wild will not be harmless.

Look at your house with an objective eye, and remove or close up anything that can spell trouble for a bird. It would be a shame to nurse even one purple martin back to health to see it lost to an accident before it can once again take to the sky.

3. Force-feed each bird until it learns to accept food on its own. Nestlings usually will start accepting food voluntarily more quickly than older birds that have learned the fear reaction.

To force-feed, hold the bird with one hand and open its bill with the other. When holding the bird, be very careful because the eyes are located close to the hinges of the bill, where your fingers will be located. A large kitchen matchstick or blunted toothpick is handy for prying open the bill and offering the food item. Place the food well back in the throat and close the bill.

4. Feed often. Martins need small, frequent feedings to provide enough nutrition without overloading their digestive systems. A baby should be offered as much food as it will take. Although many martins have been raised by feeding only every hour or even every two hours, ideally they should be fed every 30 minutes all day long. They should be fed as much as they will take and this typically is 3-4 pea-sized pellets or medium-sized insects. A typical martin will consume 70 such items a day to maintain weight. A malnourished one will need 100 items per day.

5. Use high protein food. These are insect-eaters, so their systems are adapted to mostly protein and have little tolerance for fat.

Carlyle Rogillio, who authored the **Purple Martin Rehabilitation Manual** for the Wild Bird Rehabilitation Center in New Orleans, spelled out some ideal diet factors for young purple martins:

"Science Diet Lite, "feline maintenance," dry pellets soaked in water is very close to being the one best food for a proper martin diet. It is high in protein, low in fat, and has a good calcium-phosphorus ratio. Science Diet is available at pet stores. High protein, dry dog food pellets can be substituted if Science Diet Lite is not available.

"A vitamin-mineral supplement can be made by mixing equal parts, about 1/4-teaspoon, of bone meal (calcium and phosphorus), powdered vitamins (Vionate is good), and brewer's yeast. Each of these can be obtained from a pet shop, except that brewer's yeast is easier found in health food stores. At each feeding, one of the Science Diet pellets can be dipped in the vitamin-mineral mixture.

"Mealworms are a very good food for martins. Once they learn to feed themselves, they will choose mealworms over all other food. The mealworms should be offered from a shallow dish with a one-inch rim so they can't crawl out. Place some of the vitamin-mineral mixture above the dish. The mealworms, crawling through the mixture, will get almost enough on them to supplement what is lacking from a diet of just mealworms. Mealworms can be obtained from a pet shop, from a zoo, or ordered from a supplier.

"Meat pellets made from choice, lean (no fat), raw, ground beef are a good food. It should be fresh, not out of the refrigerator for more than two or three hours. Boiled egg yolk can also be mixed into the pellets. One pellet at each feeding can be dipped into the vitamin-mineral supplement.

"Crickets are good martin food. Dip or dust them with the vitamin-mineral mixture. They are available at pet shops, bait shops and zoos."

And finally, Rogillio added an important note about water.

"Do not give nestlings water. They get their liquid from their food. The hole (glottis) at the back of the tongue is the opening to the windpipe (trachea). Trying to force a bird to drink water causes it to gag, the water goes into the trachea and can drown a bird or give it pneumonia.

"After the birds fledge, a shallow water dish can be placed for them to

Young martins will quickly learn to accept food, even though they often must be force-fed at first. Harry V. Balcom of Bossier City, Louisiana, took this picture of a pair of martins that had been rescued by Mrs. T. L. Ross of Shreveport.

drink and bathe when and if they want. Some birds seldom do either."

They can be taught to eat by themselves. Place a shallow food dish in front of the bird. Then offer it a food item and when it reaches for the item drop it back into the dish. The bird will soon learn to reach into the dish for it. Others will learn from the first bird.

INJURED BIRDS

Hand-feeding adult martins that have been injured requires pretty much the same food and feeding techniques, but adults are much slower to learn to accept food voluntarily.

Injuries are difficult to heal because songbirds are so active it is tedious to immobilize the injured part long enough for it to heal. Broken wings are the biggest challenge, but they can be healed successfully.

Rogillio pointed out, however, that stress is the first thing to treat when dealing with an injured bird. Unless an open wound is present, first leave the bird alone for about 30 minutes in a quiet, warm, dark or semi-dark place. Then examine it very carefully to determine the injury.

Of the serious injuries, broken wings are the most common, and the most difficult to heal, but it can be done. The "figure-8" bandage is recommended by the New Orleans Wild Bird Rehabilitation Center.

When the wing is at rest and folded against the body, the bones are usually in good position, so the bandage should hold the wing in that position. The wrap should be snug, but not tight enough to interfere with breathing.

Using one-half-inch strips of gauze or a more professional item such as Vet-rap, first apply the figure-8 pattern to the wing itself, as shown in the sketch, then under the good wing, across the breast and around the injured wing.

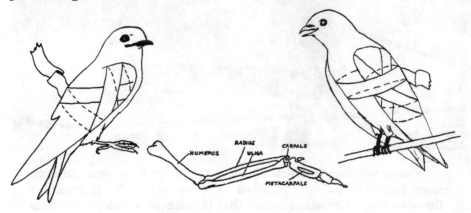

Bones should heal within two weeks. As soon as you feel this has occurred, remove the bandage and allow it to remain in a protected area for awhile longer. If the bird is recovering it will use its wings progressively more and within a week will be ready to fly.

In the case of a young bird about to fledge, you can greatly increase its chances of survival if you are able to keep it confined in a large room or confined area into which you can release a few flying insects to help the baby become familiar with its food source.

With the young bird perched, drop food to it from progressively higher levels and teach it to catch its food. Parent martins do this when the young fledglings are perched on wires during the first 2-3 days at the staging area.

You will find a fledgling may remain attached to you for a few days after you free it. It may return to alight on your shoulder after each of its short early flights. Likewise, it may return to you in the evening and expect to be taken in. But within a very few days it will be completely independent.

Watching a purple martin that you have rescued and nursed back to health take to the wing and climb into the sky is very satisfying indeed. You can almost feel a sense of exhilaration as the bird soars and dips, plunges earthward and then rises ever higher with a new sense of discovery and freedom.

You'll agree that your effort in a purple martin's behalf is worth it.

Conclusion

You have just finished reading what I believe to be the most thorough treatment ever of a single species of songbird. Some of you, I suspect, have learned more than you thought you ever wanted to know.

But it is a tribute to the endless complexity and fascination of nature that, without a doubt, you still have questions unanswered. That's nature.

Maybe when this book is next revised, it will answer still more questions, but none of us has any illusion that this or any other book can give a complete picture of nature — or even one small piece in the marvelous mosaic of natural history.

We just enjoy looking at the pieces and watching the changing patterns.

JLW

Personal Purple Martin Record
Site Information

(This page is for a permanent record of the development of
your facilities. Add information as new housing is added
or old housing removed.)

Your name:_____

Address:_____

_____

Location of colony if different:_____

_____

Type[s] of housing and year of installation of each type or unit:

_____   _____

_____   _____

_____   _____

_____   _____

_____   _____

_____   _____

_____   _____

_____   _____

General notes on this set-up:_____

_____

_____

_____

_____

_____

_____

_____

_____

_____

_____

_____

Personal Purple Martin Record
Annual Record

(For keeping a record of dates, procedures, and events you may find useful to recall.)

Year:_____ Scout date:_____ "Permanent" arrivals:_____

First hatched:_____ First fledged:_____ Last departures:_____

Total fledged:_____ Total nesting pairs:_____

What sparrow and/or starling control was used?_____

_____

_____

What parasite control was used?_____

_____

_____

Any predator problems? _____

_____

_____

Other notes on season: _____

_____

_____

_____

_____

_____

_____

_____

_____

_____

_____

_____

_____

_____

Personal Purple Martin Record
Annual Record

(For keeping a record of dates, procedures, and events you
may find useful to recall.)

Year:_____ Scout date:_____ "Permanent" arrivals:_____

First hatched:_____ First fledged:_____ Last departures:_____

Total fledged:_____ Total nesting pairs:_____

What sparrow and/or starling control was used?_____

_____

_____

What parasite control was used?_____

_____

_____

Any predator problems? _____

_____

_____

Other notes on season: _____

_____

_____

_____

_____

_____

_____

_____

_____

_____

_____

_____

_____

Personal Purple Martin Record
Annual Record

(For keeping a record of dates, procedures, and events you
may find useful to recall.)

Year:_____ Scout date:_____ "Permanent" arrivals:_____

First hatched:_____ First fledged:_____ Last departures:_____

Total fledged:_____ Total nesting pairs:_____

What sparrow and/or starling control was used?_____

_____

_____

What parasite control was used?_____

_____

_____

Any predator problems? _____

_____

_____

Other notes on season: _____

_____

_____

_____

_____

_____

_____

_____

_____

_____

_____

_____

_____

Personal Purple Martin Record
Annual Record

(For keeping a record of dates, procedures, and events you may find useful to recall.)

Year:_____ Scout date:_____ "Permanent" arrivals:_____

First hatched:_____ First fledged:_____ Last departures:_____

Total fledged:_____ Total nesting pairs:_____

What sparrow and/or starling control was used?_____

_____

_____

What parasite control was used?_____

_____

_____

Any predator problems? _____

_____

_____

Other notes on season: _____

_____

_____

_____

_____

_____

_____

_____

_____

_____

_____

_____

_____

_____

_____

Personal Purple Martin Record
Annual Record
(For keeping a record of dates, procedures, and events you may find useful to recall.)

Year:_____ Scout date:_____ "Permanent" arrivals:_____

First hatched:_____ First fledged:_____ Last departures:_____

Total fledged:_____ Total nesting pairs:_____

What sparrow and/or starling control was used?_____

_____

_____

What parasite control was used?_____

_____

_____

Any predator problems? _____

_____

_____

Other notes on season: _____

_____

_____

_____

_____

_____

_____

_____

_____

_____

_____

_____

_____

_____